Feel ıτ as a Man

A fool's guide to relationships

Nick Keith

Feel it as a Man
A fool's guide to relationships

First published in 2018 by
Panoma Press Ltd
48 St Vincent Drive, St Albans, Herts, AL1 5SJ UK
info@panomapress.com
www.panomapress.com

Cover design by Michael Inns
Artwork by Karen Gladwell

ISBN 978-1-784521-47-9

A CIP catalogue record for this book is available from the British Library.

This book is available online and in all good bookstores.

Dedication

To: Ben, Chris, Will, Hebe, Adrian, Dinah and Patrick

TESTIMONIALS

"Open and honest, with many points that the reader can learn from. Really helps explain the mystery of why men sometimes find it difficult to communicate."

JONNY ANDREWS,
AUTHORISED DISTRIBUTOR, UTILITY WAREHOUSE

"An honest exploration of feelings and learning emerging from the frontline of life experience. Nick's message is that it's never too late to bring more emotional richness to your life."

FELICITY DWYER,
CAREER COACH

"The book is a very good read and well researched."

TOM BESLY,
LANDSCAPE GARDENER

ACKNOWLEDGEMENTS

I would like to thank my whole family. I have tried to tell my family history in a straightforward way, focusing only on my own emotions – which are my responsibility. In this book, I am at pains to talk about people and events as equably and uncensoriously as possible.

First, I am grateful to my parents, Roddy and Barbara Keith, who gave me an interesting and boundary-less upbringing and nurtured my curiosity and creativity. Next, to Susie, my first wife, a marvellous mother with whom I spent 15 lively years and who brought me Ben (Benjamin Digby) and Chris (Christopher Mark); she introduced me to ballet, Fonteyn and Nureyev in *Romeo and Juliet* at the Royal Opera House, Covent Garden.

Then, my second wife Geraldine (aka Widge), an equally marvellous mother who, in 30 unforgettable years of marriage, gave me the gifts of good friends, good humour and great children – Will (William Richard) and Hebe (Hebe Victoria). I love all my children in equal measure; and I respect and honour both my wives, although I played a full part in burying the key to love and happiness.

I am also thankful for my three gorgeous granddaughters: Ella and Thea, daughters of Ben and Anna; and baby Hermione Charlotte, born on 1 January 2018 to Chris and Martha. My family scene was also blessed with brothers and sisters-in-law (Chris and Honor Vane, and Jane Onslow), who are all good friends.

Thank you to the 'half' side of the family, who have played a full part in my life: Adrian and Dinah, my lovely half-brother and sister in Canada; Barbour half-brothers, the late Bobby and his wife Julie, and Patrick, and his wife Clare; and their families. They have all given great support, good humour, and a fine sense of family values.

I could not have drafted and finished *Feel it as a Man* without Mindy Gibbins-Klein, the Book Midwife, who has guided and supported my work in the birth of this book; and also to the Panoma Press team of designers, copy editors, proofreaders, production managers, and marketers. For their patience and invaluable comments, I would like to thank my select group of readers, who provided most useful feedback.

All these people and lots of friends and acquaintances have been in my thoughts and sustained me during the creative process.

Celebrating my 70th (left to right): Ben, Anna, Chris, Will, Ella, Hebe, Patrick, Me holding Mouse and Thea, and Clare

CONTENTS

INTRODUCTION

When I told a friend that I was writing a book about men and their feelings, she looked at me quizzically and with eyebrows raised. "Do men have feelings?" she said, only half in jest.

The answer is that men do have feelings, but many of us have difficulty accessing and expressing them. The difference between the genders, for me, is that many women tend to talk instinctively to each other about their emotional problems, while many men do not. Certainly, that has been my problem in life.

In my experience, western men grow up with phrases like 'Big boys don't cry', 'Be a man', and 'Man up' ringing in their ears. And this book is largely about my experience. It was prompted by a rush of events in 2017, including divorce, my 70th birthday, and the adventure of a lifetime in India and Australia.

The times of separation and travel left me plenty of time to think about my lot and about my feelings. I have experienced desperately sad moments and exhilaratingly happy ones. That's life, but I feel happier generally and in a better place to achieve my goals of being more open, vulnerable, and communicative.

In life, my emotional empathies have settled in a place described by Julian Barnes in *The Noise of Time*, his excellent 2016 novel about Shostakovich. Barnes writes of Shostakovich: "He felt powerful emotions but had never become skilled at expressing them.

"Even at a football match he rarely yelled and lost control of himself like everyone else; he was content with the quiet annotation of a player's skill or lack of it... but he knew he was a shy and anxious person..."

That sums up perfectly how I have felt when faced with emotions or watching a football match. I'm a bigger fan of watching football than dealing with feelings.

While I don't recall ever feeling anxious or unhappy for long, I have taught myself to retreat unconsciously behind a wall of silent observation, contributing when I have felt safe (if at all), especially in my private life and personal relationships.

I taught myself the wrong way, or the fool's way, to treat women, and that has made it very hard for me to sustain relationships. I write that without rancour – it's a sad fact. And I'm coming to terms with it. Anyway, I've 'done it my way', the wrong way, and made mistakes aplenty. Or, as Frank Sinatra might have sung in 'My way – the wrong way':

I've lived a life that's full
I've travelled each and every shy way.
But more, much more than this,
I did it the wrong way.

Mistakes, I've done some poo
But then again, too much to mention.
I didn't do what I had to do
And saw it through without emotion.

I mistook each charted course
Each fateful step along the byway.
And more, much more than this
I did it the wrong way.

Yes, there were times, I'm sure you knew,
When I bit off more than I could chew
And through it all, when there was doubt
I f*cked it up and shat it out.
I ducked it all, and I stood small
And did it my way.

A year of discovery

As I have said, my own feelings surfaced from a deep dive in 2017. It was indeed a time of noise, rather than a *Noise of Time*, a momentous year for me, which saw (in roughly chronological order):

JANUARY
An agreed separation from my wife Geraldine and filing for divorce.

FEBRUARY
The planning of a trip of a lifetime to India and Australia in the autumn and buying the tickets.

MARCH
My 70th birthday, celebrated with a family lunch at home.

A hip operation, the first one on my right leg but the fifth in all.

APRIL
A move to temporary rented accommodation in Winchester.

MAY
The completion of the sale of our home in West Sussex.

JUNE
A wonderful summer birthday party with family and friends in London, organised by my four children.

JULY

Glorious Goodwood, my favourite horse racing festival.

AUGUST

A move to full-time rented accommodation in Winchester.

OCTOBER

Departure for Delhi. Travelling by train and plane from Delhi to Goa in a group.

A week touring Kerala with a personal driver.

NOVEMBER

A flight to Australia in November to attend the Melbourne Cup horse race, now my second favourite horse racing festival.

A week's visit to Sydney.

Transfer to Brisbane for one of the highlights of my 6-week trip, the first Ashes Test match between Australia and England.

End November: Return home to the UK.

DECEMBER

My first Christmas unattached for more than 30 years (with my grandchildren and their parents).

* January 2018: Divorce, decree nisi, became absolute.

At the Melbourne Cup in November 2017

'Big boys don't cry'

Many feelings have risen to the surface during this crowded year. Submerged for so long, the best part of a lifetime, these feelings have been forced up by two factors: becoming single again, and travel, which broadens and concentrates the mind. Given plenty of time to think about my emotions, I have wondered where my life went awry with two failed marriages. Yet, in many other ways, I still felt positive about my present and future.

The most important development was giving myself more time to get in touch with my feelings. Like many men, I have found huge difficulty in accessing my emotions throughout my life, and I have tended to brush them away. This fact alone has prevented me from being open, true and vulnerable, which I now know are three of the key attributes for a fulfilling emotional life.

People have probably known me more as a pensive than an obviously passionate man. And that could be applied to many men of my generation, the post-war 'baby boomers'.

We grew up in the grey shadow of the Second World War when boys were told to be brave – 'you mustn't be a sissy', and all that. So I learned to be 'strong', which meant that I lost the skill to find and express my feelings easily. Deep inside were emotions, which my ego, or inner critic, fought hard to keep suppressed – and usually won.

I did have feelings. It was just that my emotions had become inaccessible – or I had made them so – at an early age, when my mind had set up a series of barriers. It was the ego's undirected and undetected method to protect me from the perceived dangers of the world of emotions.

The ego locked my feelings behind an iron curtain. That's the best way I can explain my process. But this was false and counter-productive.

Why did that process become a habit? I knew it was a combination of family, upbringing, peers, boarding school, society, and my own perceptions, or rather misunderstandings. But I had not identified which of these factors was all-important.

People's characters are said to form largely by the time they are five years old, certainly before they are 10. A childish misinterpretation of a single event, which may be apparently insignificant at the time, can leave a lasting impression.

Anyway, the experiences of 2017, some 60 years on from my childhood, left me with a mission to continue to examine some of the evidence from past events. In this book, I have tried to capture the maelstrom of events, experiences and feelings in my life.

This is partly my anthology of emotions; my memoir of feelings. It is also a celebration of vivid memories.

What I've Learnt / This Much I Know

The magazines of *The Times* (Saturday) and *The Observer* (Sunday) have weekly one-page features where celebrities discuss events which have impacted on them. Their respective titles are *What I've Learnt* and *This Much I Know*. Each feature covers personal experiences and readers take from them what they choose.

That's the intention of this book. The aim is to interweave a record of my life experiences with a discussion of my feelings – the outcome is both factual and emotional.

What I've Learnt

1. To become aware of feelings and to express them.

2. To appreciate that feelings have many different aspects and interpretations.

3. To be open, honest and vulnerable, and therefore wholehearted.

4. To speak what you think and what you feel and accept feedback.

5. To invest time, effort and care to improve communication skills and relationships.

6. To embrace family and friends and community as the most valuable assets.

7. To find out what really drives you and discover your own special niche in life.

As I'm no expert, I want to share information which has come my way in the process, before and during writing *Feel it as a Man*

– through other people, events, books, films, music, talks, radio, TV, and videos. Some of these have resonated with my search and seemed to have been sent to me by the universe to help at exactly the right time when I was struggling with the writing process. These stories interest me and illuminate the world and the countries and communities we live in, and the people connected to us.

The planning process started in December 2017, when I heard a programme about masculinity presented by Jenni Murray on BBC Radio 4's *Woman's Hour* – one of my favourite radio programmes with so many useful insights for men. She asked a group of men at the beginning of the programme: "What's it like growing up as a man and how will this generation cope with it?"

The discussion got me thinking about my understanding of masculinity and what it meant to me to be a man. I was struck by the comments of one of the guests, Ross Raisin, who has written a novel about a gay footballer called *A Natural*. Here is his description of growing up and living as a man:

"Every man has a lot of different masculinities inside him that co-exist continually. There are challenges and joys to all of those masculinities. Today there is an increasing acknowledgement of it."

Then in January, during the first week of writing my initial draft, I read a newspaper preview of *Oz the Great and Powerful*, a 2013 film to be shown on TV. This described the film as a "respectful, imaginative and witty prequel" to the classic *Wizard of Oz* (from 1939).

"James Franco plays the Wizard as a shifty, womanising stage musician who, if he is to save Oz from its witches, will have to do so almost in spite of himself," according to the preview. (Just as it should be, then!)

The film is about "characters discovering in themselves those qualities which they had all along." This gave me hope that writing the book would help me discover things about myself and the world, which I had denied, buried or ignored and maybe, just maybe, help others.

As I have said, I am not an expert on feelings, so my stories and observations may not necessarily reveal any great truths. I am trying hard to become more knowledgeable about myself and to listen more carefully to others.

On the key topic of feelings, a few years ago I came across Brené Brown's celebrated TED Talk about the importance of being vulnerable and open-hearted. While working on the final draft I discovered, almost by accident, two more fascinating TED talks: one by the British neuroscientist Dr Alan Watkins, who differentiates between emotions and feelings (maintaining that on average humans may develop only nine feelings, while potentially we have 34,000 open to us); the other revelation was by American psychologist Dr Joan Rosenberg with her strategy for accepting and mastering feelings.

Chapter 3 on Feelings will discuss the findings of these three experts in greater detail. Meanwhile, remember my watchwords: This Much I Know; and What I've Learnt.

Notes on the title and subtitle

The title of this book is deliberately taken from *Macbeth*, one of Shakespeare's most bloody and misogynistic plays, exploring the gender differences and up-ending some of the assumptions about the roles of men and women. That is Shakespeare's viewpoint in this play I hasten to add, not mine.

The usurper Macbeth is seduced into mayhem and manslaughter by his ambitious wife, Lady Macbeth. First, she bids him to seize the Scottish throne by murdering the king, Duncan, and then Macbeth becomes part of a cycle of killing and chaos which takes the place of peace and order. In *Macbeth,* the gender roles of men and women are confused. Whenever Macbeth and Lady Macbeth talk about manhood, violence follows. They both equate masculinity with aggression and violence, which are paramount in the play.

First, Lady Macbeth manipulates her husband by questioning his manhood, wishing that she could be 'unsexed'. And Macbeth says that a woman like her should give birth only to boys. Then Lady Macbeth goads her husband to murder Duncan, the king. After that, Macbeth pressures the men he gets to kill his fellow soldier Banquo by questioning their manhood.

The aggression of the female characters goes against expectations of how women behave. The women who have roles as sources of violence and evil are:

a) The witches, whose prophecies help to fuel Macbeth's ambitions and encourage his violent behaviour;

b) Lady Macbeth, who provides the wit and the will to her husband's murderous plotting.

Her behaviour suggests that women can be just as cruelly vindictive as men – a view which was borne out by the experiences of my father in the Second World War (related later). Lady Macbeth deceives and manipulates to achieve her objectives – rather than acting violently herself – and eventually, she kills herself.

Towards the end of the play, masculinity is redefined. Malcolm encourages Macduff to take the news of the murders of his wife and child in 'manly' fashion – by having his revenge on Macbeth. But Macduff suggests this is a false understanding of masculinity.

Malcolm: "Dispute it like a man."

Macduff: "I shall do so.

But I must also feel it as a man." (*Macbeth*, Act 4 scene 3).

And in the subtitle, *A fool's guide to relationships*, I'm thinking of the Shakespearean fool, as described by the Royal Shakespeare Company in notes on *King Lear*: "The Fool acts as a commentator on events and is one of the characters who is fearless in speaking the truth."

Well, this book is my truth anyway. And I delivered my final manuscript to the publisher on 23 April, the date of Shakespeare's birthday and St George's day. So come with me to boldly go, on the Starship Manhood, into the emotional universe as I set out to *Feel it as a Man: A fool's guide to relationships*.

Nick Keith
23 April 2018

Many men find communication hard

"Communication is a skill that you can learn. It's like riding a bicycle or typing. If you're willing to work at it, you can rapidly improve the quality of every part of your life."

BRIAN TRACY

What I've Learnt

- Clear and open communication is absolutely vital in everything we do
- Listen carefully to what the other person is saying to achieve true communication
- Some people may disconnect and become uncommunicative in challenging situations
- Men and women may have misunderstandings, but they don't speak different languages

What separates humans from other animals – herds of cattle, flocks of birds and schools of fish – is their natural gift of being able to speak and understand complex languages. So they have more sophisticated methods of communicating with each other than other species.

However, some of us never learn the skill exactly as Brian Tracy describes. The ability to communicate does not mean that humans truly hear and understand each other well. Many of us are poor at communicating. That certainly includes me. Having reached the age of 70, and been consistently average to poor as a communicator, I have realised how counter-productive to everyone that has been. Why did I, and so many others, reach a dead end and become disconnected?

After all, I have enjoyed jobs in the communications industry all my working life. My career has included journalism, publishing and marketing, which all require communication skills. In my last salaried job before I retired, I was the communications director of a marketing company. I launched three community magazines as part of that job, so I was in close touch with local people.

However, my communication skills were single-tracked. They did not extend from the professional to the personal sphere. Recent insights have opened my mind to some of the gaps in my personal and emotional development, which have hindered my powers of communication – and even stopped them completely. Now I seek to regain connections.

"Effective communication involves two separate functions," writes John Karter, a UKCP registered psychotherapist, in his book *Psychology of Relationships: A Practical Guide*. He adds: "To have genuine significance, these two functions should be seen as inseparable and complementary. However, to maintain a healthy relationship, listening is the greater, more rewarding skill, because, without listening in the sense of truly trying to understand what is being said, (you) might as well be talking to a wall."

Karter's book gives these facts about listening:

- We think at 1,000-3,000 words per minute, but listen at 125-250 wpm; and, when we think we are listening, we are distracted for 75% of the time (probably working out our reply);
- Long-term, we remember only 20% of what we hear;
- Immediately after listening to someone we recall only 50% of what they have said;
- The average attention span for adults is 22 seconds.

I can smile at a cartoon which illustrates these stark facts with irony. The picture shows a secretary bursting through a door into her female employer's office and saying, "Sorry I'm late boss, but I was talking to my husband, and he wouldn't stop listening."

Karter's book tells a story about a couple who were caught up "in a seemingly endless cycle of arguing and recrimination" (just like my own parents). But their relationship blossomed when they learned to stand back from an argument, "acknowledge their own feelings of vulnerability, and, most importantly, listen to what the other person was trying to communicate instead of hitting back" (unlike my parents).

The important issue of vulnerability has become the focus of my attention since hearing Brené Brown on a TED Talk. A high-powered American academic, Brené Brown specialises in research and storytelling on social issues. She has led the way with her ground-breaking talks and books. Some 33.5 million people have viewed her TED Talk on the *Power of Vulnerability*, which she delivered in Houston in June 2010).

I will return to vulnerability in greater detail in Chapter 3 about feelings.

The early years

Jolly sailor, aged 5

As I wrote in the Introduction, I go along with the idea that one incident in a child's early life, which may appear insignificant, can have a huge impact on their psyche – on their beliefs about themselves and the world around them, and on their sense of self-worth. That incident will condition how they feel, communicate, and react to others and to events.

This negative experience leaves a deep scar, so the child learns to hold back his or her emotional development. Maybe the child was not picked up when crying, or a precious toy was taken away. I'm not a psychologist, and I have never been sure what the answer is. But I have a theory, and I'll come back to that.

In the early years of my life, I remember feeling free of inhibition. I'm a naturally positive, 'glass half full' sort of person. If I didn't get my way, sometimes I would throw terrible

24

tantrums, and roll on the ground, sobbing. I could hear my mother say, "Just leave him, let him be". And soon I had forgotten what I was howling about, gave up, and got up from the floor.

Communicating is a process

American author and businessman Paul J. Meyer, who founded the Success Motivation Institute in 1960, said, "Communication – the human connection – is the key to personal and career success." I, like some men and women of my generation, did not heed these wise words.

Communication involves dialogue and listening.

Instead of personal communication, I chose the path of disconnection. At university, my song of choice was Simon and Garfunkel's *I am a rock, I am an island ... and a rock feels no pain, and an island never cries ...*

Some men, and women, can become uncommunicative in challenging situations and shut down completely. I know I have done that with both my wives and also with my children to a certain extent. Disconnection and isolation make it harder to have adult communication, and personal discussions with family and friends.

Men can also isolate themselves, listening to their own voices. They get set in their ways and unbending in their opinions. This makes them blind to reality on the one hand and to their true worth on the other. At the pub, at a party, or in the sporting locker room, men's conversation often turns to sport, politics, and work, but rarely involves problems with personal relationships, apart from the odd grumble. Where men and women differ lies in the fact that communication, talking and sharing, seems to be a more feminine gift.

Having found myself at a loss at what to say in many different scenarios, for fear of saying the wrong thing, I have tended to say nothing at all. Sometimes, I have launched a vicious, uncalled-for, pre-emptive attack. And that behaviour has been shameful and cowardly – one of my most regrettable failures in life.

Breakdown in communication

"The single biggest problem in communication is the illusion that it has taken place."

GEORGE BERNARD SHAW

That is also true for me. Often, I have kidded myself that I have shared a personal opinion or a feeling with a wife or a loved one and sworn blind that I have done so. But, in reality, those opinions and emotions have remained buried and unspoken.

The failure to talk openly about feelings, aggravations and fears is bound to lead to a breakdown in communication, and ultimately in the relationship itself. My own experience is summed up by John Karter, who writes:

"An unwillingness to listen, or more accurately to hear, what the other person is trying to get across creates a vicious cycle of resentment, an even greater restriction on communication, and, eventually a total shutdown."

Indeed, that is so true of both my marriages. It's easy to be wise after the event, but if I had heard and heeded the advice of others, and listened with due care and attention, things in my personal life might have been so different.

Language barriers

However, I don't believe that there are language barriers between men and women, that they speak different languages, that

Men are from Mars and Women are from Venus, as American relationship counsellor John Gray wrote in his best-selling 1992 book of the same name.

It just seems that way sometimes, and that has led to thoughtless assumptions by the men and women who have read his book (more than 50 million copies sold). In my view, the book was stereotypical of gender and people, and not always helpful to understanding how men and women are.

Gray stated that men and women are from different planets spiritually, which has prevented them from speaking the same language; and they also have different social mores. He popularised the notion that many men when challenged or stressed, retreat and 'go into a cave', while women tend to talk and have dialogue. While it's important to say that he rightly emphasised the importance of communication, I don't believe that men and women are so vastly different in their feelings – just in their ability to access them, process them, and talk about them.

The problem with Gray's idea is that there is not such a rigid division between men and women. There is certainly no one-size-fits-all answer to the subtleties of human nature. I'm sure we all know a few women who go into, or live in, a cave.

Summary

The fact that many men can't or don't articulate their feelings does NOT mean that we are from another planet and speak a different language from women. Our communication styles are different.

The big difference between the genders, as I have said, is that many women can talk, listen and have a dialogue about a wide variety of things, from the everyday to the emotionally traumatic.

Many men have not acquired this habit.

Some men like to be fixers and problem-solvers – and very often go it alone. The only conversation they have is with themselves. Or they make a statement, but they don't listen properly. If men's communication style is the problem and needs fixing, that requires understanding and dialogue. (John Karter quotes the pithy words of Jeff Daly: "Two monologues do not make a dialogue.")

In my case, I failed to develop a skill for communication at the personal level. And the older I got, my communication became more restricted, more remote, and more limited. Indeed my communication became subsumed in my writing.

Yet, the written word reduces the power, directness and intimacy of personal communication. And in my case, writing has helped me to hide my emotions.

"Writing was born as the maidservant to human consciousness, but it is increasingly becoming its master." Yuval Noah Harari in *Sapiens: A Brief History of Humankind*.

Certainly, I could be more courageous, open, and vulnerable in expressing out loud feelings: joys and sadnesses, annoyance and accord, pleasure and pain.

The next chapter looks at relationships, particularly with family and friends.

CHAPTER TWO

RELATIONSHIPS

Family, friends, loved ones

"I think for any relationship to be successful, there needs to be loving communication, appreciation, and understanding."

MIRANDA KERR

My parents, Roddy and Barbara

This Much I Know

- Children's perceptions of their situation and relationships, formed in the first five years of their lives, are likely to be misconceived
- Parents do the best they can and are not to blame for our problems
- Build and maintain relationships with care, consideration, openness, listening and love
- Relationships are important to everyone, but no generation seems to have found the secret yet

As I grew up and watched my parents' marriage founder, I was determined to make a better go of relationships. People in my generation thought they had found the key to relationships, through the open culture of the 1960s – love, peace and understanding.

We used that new-found key to try to open the door to relationships, marriage, children, and happiness – not necessarily in that order! However, a lot of us threw away the key and felt locked out or excluded through lack of communication, misperceptions, and misunderstandings. I reckon that in the early stages of a relationship I was open, but once it became settled, I cut the communication cord.

Of course, relationships start at home, and there follows a description of my impressions of my childhood ... But they are only my perceptions.

My sweet and sour home life

My early life and upbringing were neither dull nor idyllic. However, my childhood was blessed with a creative and boundary-less quality.

Yet, my parents argued and fought, verbally and physically. There was a combustible chemistry between them, and a fight broke out almost in the minute they came together. Even when I was young, I did not feel that this was a marriage made in heaven or that they should necessarily stay together.

Growing up, I gradually became uncommunicative with my nearest and dearest. I completely misunderstood my mother and failed to respect her. I only realised how insecure and unhappy she was when I was in my 30s.

Mum seemed boisterous and loud and had a quick tongue, usually behind people's backs, and especially in company with her best friend Gris (Griselda Gage). Like a golfing version of the French and Saunders jacketed country ladies, they used to sit together near the bar at the golf club or the pub berating all and sundry. It was amusing only if you weren't the butt of their jokes.

Amy Barbara Wood (Barbara) was born in 1905 brought up in a solid middle-class Yorkshire family, who had made their money from woven fabrics like bunting, and then moved out of Bradford to Ilkley in the early 20th century. She was just about the only member of the family to leave the county.

Pa, my father, James Roderick Keith (Roddy), was born in 1912 and seemed a deeply unhappy man to me. Arguably there were two reasons: his 'Victorian-style' upbringing and his early life experiences. His father Leo, a professional soldier, went to fight in the First World War from 1914 to 1916 (when he was wounded). Pa cannot have had a close connection with his father, indeed with either of his parents.

I believe he was brought up by nannies and saw little of Olga, his mother. He was sent away to prep school and was privately educated at Charterhouse. After school, he worked in Ireland for Gallagher's, the tobacco company.

When I was born, he was working in the advertising industry for J Walter Thompson, whose offices were at 40 Berkeley Square. That was the era of advertising so brilliantly captured in the TV series, *Mad Men*.

I have a clear memory of the bar where Mum and I used to meet Pa. It was called '40 Below' in Berkeley Square, and as a young lad I was treated to a special alcohol-free cocktail which the barman called a Pussyfoot Pimms.

Pa used to travel a lot on business, and there was heavy drinking for all concerned, at work and at home. His clients included the American giants Pan-Am, the airline, and Mars (which had a factory in Slough, near where we lived).

About a boy

I was born into what is now called the 'baby-boomer' generation. We benefited from being the first generation to find ourselves with some decent pocket money, the confidence supplied by our own brand of music and earnings from small jobs. And we had material stuff to spend it on, in my case mainly books, pop records, and my bicycle (later a small motorcycle).

Mum told me once that I had been named Nicholas after the son of a friend who had been killed in a motorbike accident. I made nothing of that singular piece of information. On another occasion, I have a strong memory of her saying that my father found me 'boring'. I have never forgotten that comment.

The first five years of my life were spent at Cut Mill, Puttenham, near Guildford. The house was surrounded by a lot of land with a long drive, a lake and a moat in front of the house, and the gardener's cottage across the drive opposite.

My earliest happy childhood memories include: watching the family whippets Jiminy and Pander from my pram while they chased rabbits; building a snowman in the drive; feeding the pigs at the bottom of the garden; following our gardener Jack while he mowed the lawn; and riding my precious pedal car on the patio. I also have a very strong memory of my parents shouting and screaming at each other in their bedroom across the landing from my nursery. They sounded like they were beating each other up.

This was my first encounter with adult communication, and it sounded both playful and violent at the same time. The sense of unexplained violence struck home. So, that chimes in with the knowledge that the first five years of my life had a massive impact on me. It was when I learned to walk, talk and think (mainly selfishly, of course).

However, there is no sign of trauma in my remembered feelings of the time or in family photos of me. They show a cheerful, smiling fair-haired boy with freckles and dimples, often sitting in his pedal car on the patio at Cut Mill.

My two older half-brothers, Bobby and Patrick Barbour, were brought up alongside me, so I knew them from birth. They weren't at home much because they were older than me by 16 and 13 years respectively: Bobby, who was at Winchester College and then in National Service, used to tease his toddler brother mercilessly with a football; and Patrick went to Eton the year I was born.

When Patrick was 17, he had a motorbike, and I badgered Mum to be allowed to sit on the front and be taken for a ride to the end of the drive. After what seemed like forever to a five-year-old, permission was finally granted, and Patrick drove me out of the Cut Mill grounds.

Easy rider: aged 5 with my brother Patrick on his motorbike

I can remember clearly the thrill of sitting in front of him as we drove steadily down the long drive and then out into the open road, a narrow country lane. I fancy we stopped at a crossroads and took in a few deep breaths. Every time I hear Bob Seger's *Roll Me Away* I'm back on Patrick's bike.

Seger's super song about a biker in the American West finishes:

Stood alone on a mountain top
Starin' out at the Great Divide
I could go east; I could go west
It was all up to me to decide
Just then I saw a young hawk flyin'
And my soul began to rise
And pretty soon
My heart was singin'

Roll, roll me away
I'm gonna roll me away tonight
Gotta keep rollin', gotta keep ridin'
Keep searchin' till I find what's right
And as the sunset faded I spoke
To the faintest first starlight
And I said next time
Next time
We'll get it right.

The lyrics give me goosebumps and, although I'll never be a biker, I treasure the sentiment in the song. This short bike ride was the first of many occasions when I have felt the loving support of my half-brother Patrick. He has always backed me, but not without asking positive questions. His innate sense of optimism and adventure have continued to enthuse me. Patrick, I owe you a great deal. Thank you.

On the move

Then, when I was five, we suddenly upped sticks and moved from Cut Mill to Ascot, to a much smaller rented house opposite the Berkshire Golf Club. Within a year we had moved again, to a roomier apartment nearby, in a big place which had been converted into flats. Little did I know that this coincided with the arrival of Pa's new offspring, my half-brother Adrian.

In the 1950s, my father had an affair with his secretary Audrey, and they had two children: Adrian was born in 1952 and Dinah in 1953. This was at the dawn of my consciousness of life, and for almost another 10 years I was unaware that Adrian and Dinah were my half-siblings, who have since become warm family friends.

Adrian, Audrey, Me and Dinah in Toronto, early 2000s

I used to see something of them when I was young, as they lived close by. I thought they were cousins, and my mother used to babysit for them sometimes. I discovered the truth only when I was in my mid-teens, and I certainly bore no ill will towards them.

The families went their separate ways in the 1960s when Pa moved back permanently to Dublin, where he grew up and which he felt was his natural home. He died there in 1969 at the age of 57.

Back then, Pa divided his leisure time between the two households. And the rumble of angry dispute still hung over the encounters between my parents.

I can't say that the move affected me much, as our new home (Herons Brook) had a large garden, big enough to meet the needs of a young adventurer, who spent much of his time climbing trees and playing football on his own – scoring goals for England.

There was a significant other who protected me from any potential harm in this period. That was Nanny, Caroline Lewis, who had been with us since my birth. A spinster in her 60s, her 'babies' had been the children she had looked after since going into service as a teenager.

Nanny provided a hard rock against the potentially cruel world, and a soft pillow for me to cushion my inner space. If ever anyone, my father included, made a snide remark, she used to throw her

Mum, Granny Wood, and Nanny in Ilkley, late 1950s

head back slightly and give them a dismissive look. She lovingly threw cricket balls at me in the garden at Herons Brook, while I batted and fielded at the same time for Yorkshire and England.

For a while Nanny and I shared a bedroom at Herons Brook. The third bedroom belonged to Patrick who was still a teenager and had not left home yet. After leaving school, he went travelling in America, selling encyclopaedias and vacuum cleaners. I cherished his long airmail letters on blue paper with multiple folds.

When Patrick came back to the UK, he left home to get a job, and I inherited his bedroom. Nanny stayed on to help look after Granny (Olga) Keith who had moved into a neighbouring flat.

Role models

My family role models were strong-minded and vociferous. Both my parents were forthright. They seemed to be popular down at the local pub and at the golf club, which is where I saw them at play most as I grew older.

So, we had a noisy and confident household, where I was encouraged to play my part in proceedings, memorably when I was at prep school and was badgered to tell ribald and rude schoolboy jokes at the Christmas dinner table.

When I was 13, we moved to New Mile Corner, Ascot. The house overlooked the straight mile on the famous royal racecourse, where the track used to cross the main road (and turf was put down on the tarmac during race meetings). Today the racetrack crosses the road over a bridge with traffic passing underneath.

Olga came to live with us in a granny annexe which was built for her. Audrey, Adrian and Dinah also moved into the area, a few miles away. While I heard about them in snatches, we rarely came face to face, and I still thought they were 'distant cousins'.

Before long, I guessed the truth, and my mother's best friend Gris confirmed the reality when I asked her on a memorable car journey – through Windsor Great Park, as I recall. I really didn't know what to think or feel. Was it such a big deal? I did not harbour any negative feelings, reasoning that I had no control over the situation. I remember that I shrugged away my feelings.

Perplexed more than hurt, I now knew why Pa spent only half his time with us. Besides, the relationship between my parents was becoming increasingly strained. Meetings quickly turned into arguments, usually about petty things. Their relationship seemed like an unholy cocktail of incendiary chemical elements, likely to explode at the slightest touch.

Larkin about

For a great part of my life, I accepted as gospel Philip Larkin's famous poem,

This Be The Verse?

They f*ck you up, your mum and dad.
  They may not mean to, but they do.

They fill you with the faults they had
  And add some extra, just for you.

But they were f*cked up in their turn
  By fools in old-style hats and coats,

Who half the time were soppy-stern
  And half at one another's throats.

Man hands on misery to man.
  It deepens like a coastal shelf.

Get out as early as you can,
  And don't have any kids yourself.

Larkin, a cricket and sports fan like me, is seen by some as a national treasure. He became the 'best-loved English poet' after the war. His sad, insular style suited the national melancholy.

The website of the Philip Larkin Society (philiplarkin.com) includes a critique of him in a 1993 TV documentary by Terry Eagleton. (YouTube: *Without Walls: J'Accuse Philip Larkin.*) Larkin is condemned as a 'death-obsessed, emotionally-retarded misanthropist who had the impudence to generalise his own fears and failings to the way things are'.

Eagleton's documentary has interesting insights on the English character and mood immediately after the war. Dogged by pessimism, lugubriousness, and insularity, British society was anti-intellectuals, anti-heroes, and anti-foreigners. "Larkin could find words for things but not for people," according to Eagleton.

The 1950s and early 1960s, when Larkin prospered, were in my formative early years. This was an era when the prevailing mood was pessimistic. However, my parents did not seem pessimistic, and I now believe they did the best they could.

Context is important. Many mothers and fathers were older because of the War, and they had been brought up by parents who had inherited Victorian values and parenting methods. My paternal grandparents were from the Victorian age with traditional values of parenting: 'Children should be seen and not heard'. They were almost certainly distant from their own children.

However, they were not fools and, in my experience, neither were they 'at each other's throats'. I remember my paternal grandfather Leo Keith as a courteous, upright and noble man. A true gentleman who had been invalided out of the First World War with wounds. He died when I was eight in 1955.

For many years his widow, my grandmother Olga, lived either very close to us or in the same house. She was a warm and loving grandmother, with whom I used to have pillow fights as a child. Nothing Victorian in that!

Going back to my parents' experience of childhood, their formative period was the First World War and the Roaring Twenties. Their early lives were spent in retreat from the noise of the First World War; then came the 1920s, when the world moved into the age of jazz, with cocktails, laughter and the Charleston; the 'Age of Excess'.

That was followed by the Great Depression, the General Strike, and the Wall Street Crash in the 1930s – when Hollywood was born and, musically, swing replaced the jitterbug. Then the clouds of world war descended on the world once more.

The 1940s, the years dominated by the Second World War, were dubbed as the *Age of Anxiety*, by the poet W H Auden. And the 1950s were years of post-war frugality, moderation and making do – The 'Age of Conformity'.

My mother seemed such a free spirit that I guessed her upbringing was slightly less formal. To me, she appeared to have all the attributes and foibles of a 1920s 'flapper girl' – dancing and drinking in a never-ending whirl of nonsensical superficiality (as I saw it). That was my childlike perception of her, and I was wrong.

I never knew her father, Geoffrey Wood, who died in 1946 the year before I was born. But I remember Granny Wood (Jenny) who lived in a large house above Ilkley near the famous moor. She was a gentle Yorkshire lass, who lived until she was 90 and still cycled into town in her 80s. I enjoyed staying with her, and I have inherited her diary, which is full of things, not people – such as getting up early to clean the house before the cleaner arrived!

Family relationships

These undoubtedly have a huge bearing on people as they grow up. After all, it is our childhood perceptions and misconceptions which colour our lives and make the deepest impression on us.

My relationship with my parents was distant. I chose to be distant from my mother for my own selfish reasons. But the distance from my father was more of his making, and I was too young and too reserved to bridge it. Indeed, I always sensed that he was nervous or fearful of (the responsibility?) fatherhood. Pa and I barely had a proper conversation in the 22 years I knew him. In all the photographs taken of him in later life, during the 25 years after the Second World War, he looked decidedly downcast.

"Give peace a chance"

Julian Lennon summed up poor communication between fathers and sons when he said of his Beatle father, John:

"Dad could talk about peace and love out loud to the world, but he could never show it to the people who supposedly meant the most to him: his wife and son. How can you talk about peace and love and have a family in bits and pieces – no communication, adultery, divorce? You can't do it, not if you're being true and honest with yourself."

Married life

That brings me to my two marriages. First, I honour and respect both my wives, Susie and Geraldine, belatedly perhaps. I realise that my love, honour and respect was hardly revealed to them when we were married.

Susan Libby Vane and I were married in October 1969 at Remenham Church, near Henley-on-Thames. I felt happy and thrilled that I had found a relationship and a family to replace my experiences as I grew up.

I was not all disheartened that my half-brother Bobby arrived drunk at the wedding. The man who drove the family down from Chiswick in a hired limo said to him, "Sir, I have taken many a person away from a wedding in your condition, but never to a wedding." In the church, Bobby nudged me from behind and hissed conspiratorially, "There's still time to get out!"

In vino veritas? Not at all as, in my mind, I was happy, and felt happily married for 13 years. Susie and I were already living together in a rented flat just off the Fulham Road, London, with her brother Chris. I was devoted to the Vane family who seemed to offer many of the things I had missed in my own – size, scope, togetherness and a dream island in Scotland (Eilean Shona, which used to host J M Barrie).

As well as three siblings (Fiona, Chris and Charlie), Susie had an added ingredient in the family cocktail. Her godfather Reggie Rotheroe had lived with the Vane family for more than 20 years. Her parents, Digby and Kay, ran their company in Perivale, north-west London, and Reggie had his own business nearby.

During the war, Reggie separated from his wife and went to stay with Digby and Kay 'for a weekend, which turned into a lifetime'. He had a great sense of humour and was an inventive engineer who created and made key components for aircraft radar equipment; Digby ran an engineering business. They both made crucial contributions to the war effort, so there was no question of them having to fight. Besides, Reggie was asthmatic, and Kay always said she would have shot her husband in the knee if he had been called up.

The two men got on well. Kay was a strong woman who enjoyed the devoted, practical and organisational virtues of her husband, which complemented Reggie's 'softer' relationship skills. They made a united trio, and Kay always denied strongly that there had ever been anything untoward in their triangular relationship.

I enjoyed their company, their lifestyle, and my role as their son-in-law. Together they were known as 'the Big Three'.

In 1970, Chris, Susie, and I bought jointly a four-storey house in Gloucester Avenue, Camden. The house was close to pretty Primrose Hill and cost us less than £10,000 – which some older people said was scandalously expensive. Our neighbours included the leading fashion photographer David Bailey, so there was a constant stream of models on the street where we lived.

We had the top maisonette, while Chris occupied the lower two floors with the garden. I remember the night when we entertained Chris and his future wife Honor to dinner. After they were married the four of us lived happily together for 12 years.

I used to drive to work at the two newspapers where I trained as a journalist, in Watford and then Hemel Hempstead, while Susie took our pug dog to her job at a flat-sharing agency in Piccadilly and Chris worked for the family firm in Perivale.

In 1972 my journalist's training was completed, and Susie and I decided to go on an adventure around Europe and to the Middle East in a camper van and finish up in Egypt in the Valley of the Kings, before having children. So I resigned my job in the early summer and settled down to do some route planning and watching the Munich Olympics on TV.

A huge shadow was cast over those Games on
5 September when Palestinian terrorists took
hostage 11 Israeli athletes, coaches and a West
German policeman in the Olympic Village. Two
hostages were killed on the spot, and the rest died,
as well as three terrorists, during a botched rescue
attempt at the local military airport.

This was the infamous Munich Massacre, which I
watched with anguish on TV and was not eclipsed
by the sporting achievements of Mark Spitz with
his seven swimming gold medals; Soviet gymnast
Olga Korbut, three golds; and runners Lasse Virén,
from Finland, and Valeriy Borzov, Soviet Union,
with two golds each on the athletics track.

That autumn I was also privileged to take Alexander, Chris and
Honor's son and my new nephew, for walks on Primrose Hill in
his buggy.

In October, Susie and I set off in our 'combi', a converted
Luton van. We were not as adventurous as we had planned.
Having covered most of Western Europe and reached Istanbul,
the situation in the Middle East erupted and became bellicose
before the outbreak of the 1973 war between Israel and its Arab
neighbours, mainly Egypt. So our original destination, the Valley
of the Kings, was ruled out.

In 1974, the four of us sold our home in Primrose Hill and
moved to a large Buckinghamshire place – The Glebe House,
Dinton, near Aylesbury – which easily divided into two. Our son
Ben was born that September.

It's hard to remember feelings going back more than 30 years. But I know I was emotionally absent if physically present. At home, I enjoyed being a hands-on father and working hard in the large garden, growing vegetables. Christopher, our second son, was born in 1976 after some complications, as Susie and the medics had a struggle to stop him being born very prematurely. Eventually, he emerged into this world after 32 weeks in the womb and weighing 4lbs (two bags of sugar).

The best part of those early years of fatherhood was that I got to know my sons. As I didn't have to leave for work until lunchtime, I could play with them and take them to the local playground. But I was not involved from midday to late at night as I was working shifts for *The Times*, first as a sub-editor and then as Sports Editor from 1979.

My job at *The Times* realised one of my dreams and passions, and I suppose it diverted my attention from Susie. Yet I thought I was being an ideal husband, allowing her freedom and being a hands-on father. We talked the talk about having an open marriage where people were free to err, but we never practised it.

I didn't see the marital breakdown and separation coming, as I was blind and revelling in my job. It never occurred to me that her relationship with Roger Hawkins, a village friend of ours, was becoming deeper. I did receive one warning, but I did not believe that my marriage was under threat, even if our relationship ties were strained.

In early 1982, my mother died of cancer. In the last six months, she had suffered from dementia and had become increasingly incoherent. After her death, I went to confirm her identity in the London hospital where she lay.

I kissed her farewell and whispered that I was sorry not to have been a more loving son. Although her death was a welcome release from her physical tribulations, it still came as a shock. At a garage near the hospital, I filled up my car with diesel instead of petrol and ruined the engine.

I felt empty at first, but sadness and shame crept in. From my point of view, the best thing was that mum did not witness the death-throes of my marriage. After much soul-searching, and many comings and goings throughout that summer, Susie and I made the sad decision to separate, an anguishing one for me. She left home with Christopher to live with Roger, while I stayed at the Glebe House. Ben was sent to boarding school.

While I could still see my children as much as I wanted, I was dreadfully hurt, feeling both abandoned and ashamed about how much I had neglected Susie. I had failed to be present for her or embrace her emotional needs. Grief poured out of me for weeks on end. Tears bucketed, although I put on a brave face whenever I saw family, friends and, particularly, my children. I had felt nothing like it since I had been 'abandoned' at prep school 27 years before.

I was as much to blame for our split as anyone – I knew that. In the autumn, I left my job at *The Times* and set up a publishing company – the conflicting factor was that Roger was a partner. I was in a complete mess, which wasn't his fault. And I poured out my tears and tribulation only to close friends.

One friend said that it had taken him four years to 'get back to normal' after the failure of his marriage. And it was a similar story for me.

During my 'recovery' period, I had one notable girlfriend, but my exit from that relationship was not my finest hour. She was good fun, and we had a lot of laughs. However, my reserved ego could not cope well enough to build a lasting relationship with her.

Of course, she was extremely upset when I told her I wanted to separate.

We had a farewell weekend in Madrid, where I thought we had a great time – which was certainly confusing for her. I guess that was because my deep-seated fear of intimacy was somehow freed when I felt detached from the relationship.

That's hard to explain – and probably looks like a masculine cop-out – although the farewell weekend was the idea of a female counsellor I was seeing at the time. I could not explain my actions. I did not know how to. I lacked the communication and emotional skills to have a proper conversation and try to explain my feelings and listen to her side of the story. You might have thought that I would have become more aware of my feelings after my experiences with Susie. Not a bit of it.

Geraldine (left) with our daughter Hebe

Geraldine Onslow and I met when we were working together for a lifestyle magazine, *London Gentleman*, in the mid-1980s. However, we did not become an 'item' until well after the magazine closed 18 months later. She was pretty and witty and well-connected, with a wide group of friends. I remember making up my mind that she was the one and pursuing her with persistence.

It's a huge pity that my persistence petered out soon after we were married. I never really talked to her about her stuff and my problems with feelings. We have two wonderful children, Will (born in 1988) and Hebe (1990), who are a great gift to us.

Will and Hebe came to realise as they grew up that their parents' marriage was in trouble. Although we thought we were doing a clever job to appear normal and together when they came home, apparently, they could spot the yawning gap between us and sense our emotional stress with each other.

In a legal sense, the separation and then divorce proceedings, which started in 2016 and were completed in 2018, were civilised. But in a spiritual sense, they were not. We went through a mediation process because we did not want to incur extra costs by using separate solicitors.

We agreed about everything except the division of the money. Geraldine was cross that I had not yielded more, while my verdict was that I had given away too much of my share of our estate. The fact that we had an unsatisfactory marriage for the best part of 30 years is a huge sadness for me and will grieve me for years to come.

Undoubtedly, I retreated to my cave, again, preferring to let things happen, or rather not happen, in our relationship. My emotions remained hard to access, and I was ever-fearful of exposing them. We gave a great deal of thought to ending the marriage before we mutually came to the conclusion that divorce was the only answer – for both of us.

'Shared custody'

Geraldine and I still see each other regularly as we share custody of our dog, Mouse, a dachshund-springer-poodle, and I hope we will remain friends. By the way, I believe pets, as well as your children, reflect well on you. And I am proud that the last two dogs we have owned have both been treasures.

From 2000-14, there was Alfie, a sprollie (springer/collie cross), and since 2016 it has been Mouse, a dachshund/springer/poodle.

Alfie with Chris (left) and Ben *Mouse at the Kennels, Goodwood House*

Children and grandchildren

Ben, born 1974, married to Anna, and their daughters Ella (B: 2005) and Thea (2008).

Chris, born 1976, married to Martha, and their daughter Hermione (B: 1 January 2018).

Will, born 1988.

Hebe, born 1990.

*Chris and Martha's wedding,
with Susie and Roger behind me in
the centre of the picture*

Hermione

Emotional war wound

This section of family relationships has to include my father's experience towards the end of the Second World War which I mentioned in the Introduction. I believe this affected his powers of love for, trust in, and connection with humanity. This, in turn, had an impact on my life and upbringing.

In April 1945, he was in the advance party which brought about the relief of Belsen concentration camp. As allied troops marched through northern Germany towards Berlin, they liberated Belsen on the way. Belsen was the camp where Anne Frank died shortly before relief arrived. It was also where a BBC film crew, including Richard Dimbleby (father of David and Jonathan), captured the horrors of the camp on a famous newsreel. This film was nearly suppressed by the broadcasting authorities back home. At first, they refused to show the film, because it revealed such brutality by the warders, including the women. But Dimbleby protested so vehemently that the BBC authorities were forced to change their minds. He recorded that "This day in Belsen was the most horrible of my life."

My father was part of the reconnaissance party which went to Belsen to assess the situation in advance of the actual relief force. What they found was horrendous: skeletal bodies piled in mass graves, and the survivors' lives hanging by a thread. And my father was one of the first to witness that terrible scene.

He rarely talked about his experiences. However, he did say that he had previously believed women to be both the fairer and kinder sex. But his beliefs were shattered when he saw the cruelty of some of the female guards at Belsen. He also came to the pessimistic conclusion that all humans, not just the Nazis, were capable of barbarity. I reckon this life experience affected my father so deeply that it helped to bring on the alcohol addiction which, in my view, contributed to his early death at the age of 57.

Five years ago, Will and I visited the camp at Belsen. Situated in unremarkable countryside in Lower Saxony near the town of Bergen, Belsen was, at various times, an internment camp, a holding camp and a recovery camp, where sick prisoners were sent to 'recuperate'. However, either they died or were shipped to the gas chambers at Auschwitz.

Although Belsen was never a death camp, some 50,000 people died there of disease, exhaustion, starvation or medical neglect. Between 1943 and 1945, when it was controlled by the SS, some 120,000 people passed through it. After the camp had been shown as an example to local German administrators and then cleared of people, it was burnt to the ground because of typhus and other diseases, and the area returned to heathland for a while.

Over the years the site has been gradually restored as a memorial – the first in Germany to commemorate the horrors of the Nazi war crimes.

Will and I were impressed by the still and peaceful layout of Belsen. Mounds with plaques recorded the number of people who had died in that spot. The large modern exhibition and document building dating from 1990 was full of young German students studying what their ancestors had done. I was pleased and encouraged to note that.

There was also a House of Silence for reflection. Reflections haunted my father for the rest of his life, I am sure. As I have said, he could not discuss or share his experiences and feelings, and I sense that his silence was somehow infectious. For further information, watch a memorable documentary on Belsen called *Night Will Fall*, a compilation of contemporary works by film-makers such as Alfred Hitchcock. You can see it on Netflix https://www.netflix.com/title/80015213/

Are relationships getting better?

When I started researching this book, I was convinced that communication and relationships were improving. However, I have just found another side to that perception.

On Valentine's Day 2016 Jay Shetty posted a video called *Relationship Goals* on YouTube. Jay, who has become one of *Forbes Magazine's* top 30 thirty-year-olds in the world, has built an international reputation and following for vlogging – inspirational videos with strong, clear messages.

He opened his video *Relationships Goals* by quoting a couple who had enjoyed a good relationship for 65 years. He asked them, how come? Then he went on,

"Their reply was quite unique.

"They said that they had lived in a time when, if something was broken, they would fix it and it would go away...

"Now people treat relationships like video games. They start playing them and, when they get bored, they quit...

"We are meant to love people and use things, but today we use people and love things...

"The way we communicate says it all: we spend more time holding our phones than holding each other...

"A lot of problems in the world would disappear if we stopped talking about each other and started talking to each other.

"If everyone started talking one on one, we could start a connection and a dialogue that helps solve the challenges of today.

"When you are young you say, 'I love you because I need you'. When you grow up, you say, 'I need you because I love you'.

"Relationships are not about compromises. They're about encouraging the other person to achieve their goals..."

In other words, the struggle for humans to communicate, have a dialogue and form relationships goes on.

'The generation that doesn't want relationships'

Jay Shetty has produced many memorable videos since, and on 15 February 2018, he posted another one. This video went viral, made the *Huffington Post* online news, and hit the pages of the *Daily Mail* newspaper.

It was called, *We're the generation that doesn't want relationships...*

Here are some extracts from his vibrant four-minute video:

"We're the generation that doesn't want relationships....

We talk and we text

We Snapchat and we sext

We hang out, and we have happy hour

We go to a bar and have a beer.

Anything to avoid having an actual date...

We forgo any chance of real connection by mutually playing games with no winner....

We need to realise that the things that are truly fulfilling all require patience.

They all require work.

They all require energy...

The problem with our generation not wanting relationships is that, at the end of the day, we actually do."

Jay's vlog was inspired by a blog by 20-something Krysti Wilkinson.

So, vloggers like Jay Shetty and Krysti Wilkinson are telling a different story.

This is most disconcerting for a baby boomer like me. You see, I thought that young people of today had found some of the answers to relationship problems, with their hanging out and constant connection through social media and modern technology.

They appeared to be able to have close relationships between genders, same gender or transgender without the whole meaning being complicated by sex, misunderstanding and jealousy. However, if Shetty and Wilkinson are right, there's still a long way to go along the Road Less Travelled, the Road to Freedom, or wherever we are heading. Surely, it's not the Road to Nowhere?

My concern is that my generation's parenting skills have proved counter-productive.

Solitude

While relationships are important, successful couples tend to have individual interests, pursuits and sense of self. Leading British psychologist Dr Anthony Storr says in his book *Solitude* that these "define identity" and "give meaning to life", as well as relationships. He also argues that "many creative activities are predominantly solitary". People must develop their imagination to adapt to the world and "some of the most profound and healing psychological experiences take place internally," he adds.

Loving communication

The quote at the beginning of this chapter refers to the need for appreciation and communication to achieve successful relationships. These are summed up in the loving words of my half-brother Adrian at my 70th birthday dinner in June 2017. At the event, guests were photographed with a Polaroid camera which produced instant pictures to stick into a commemorative album entitled 'Nick is 70' and then they added a personal caption. Here's what Adrian wrote with his photo:

> *"Nick,*
>
> *It took a lifetime to share our lives*
> *and now the love I have for you*
> *allows me to share your special day.*
>
> *I am so proud to have you as*
> *my brother to enjoy the times*
> *we get to see each other.*
>
> *Love You*
> *Adrian x"*

For me, Adrian's words bring together in a simple, personal and honest way the complicated issues of communication, family and relationships. Thank you, Adrian, for bringing me such clarity by expressing your loving sentiments.

Adrian

The next chapter enters the realm of feelings.

Discover your emotions and express them

"Vulnerability is the core of all emotions and feelings."

BRENÉ BROWN

What I've Learnt

- The fundamental importance of being vulnerable, open and honest
- The equal validity of emotional intelligence
- Embrace feelings stirred by music, books, TV, theatre and everyday experiences
- Treasure feelings, let them go and move on

The realm of feelings and emotions provides clues about how we communicate and connect. If we don't connect with our feelings, we don't communicate properly, and we disconnect from others.

What do feelings mean? It's typical of the English language that the definitions of 'emotion' and 'feeling' don't bring complete clarity to the subject.

The prime definition of emotion is 'moving out' or 'excitement', originating from French in the *Shorter Oxford*

English Dictionary (SOED). And, figuratively, it means 'any vehement or excited mental state'.

In the last 300 years, emotion has become associated with the psychological state of 'a mental feeling (of pain, desire, hope etc.) as distinct from cognitions or volitions'. From the 1840s emotional meant 'connected with the feelings or passions; liable to, or easily affected by...'

'Feeling' is defined as 'the general sense of the body; the condition of being emotional'. This 'condition' included 'sympathies and susceptibilities'. The SOED declares that it became '(after Kant) the element of pleasure or pain in any state'.

Two emotions: love and fear?

Some experts have said that there are only two emotions: love and fear. All the rest are subsidiary. But, for me, the emotional pack is much more complicated and baffling.

From a young age, having heard my parents screaming at each other, I decided to try to avoid emotions, which seemed both angry and sad. Of course, I experienced childish screaming fits of my own, as I have said, but these were different. They were sudden, explosive, uncontrolled, and self-centred. I simply had not got what I wanted, or I had been punished unfairly, as I saw it.

I reckoned that, if I could keep my feelings in balance and underground – even if they were teetering on the brink of unbalancing or surfacing – life might be easier and less painful. In football parlance, I was playing for an emotional 0-0 draw. OK, there would not be much excitement; not many shots on goal, except long range, and therefore easily dealt with by my defences.

But I would avoid the angst of fighting against the huge disappointment of big defeats and emotional relegation, or the roller-coaster excitement of battling for the title (where I might also face disappointment). Of course, life does not work out with the simplicity of a football match.

Vulnerability and wholeheartedness

How I wish I had known more about these two potential attributes in the human psyche when I was younger. But they have come into my life only recently. I have always avoided being vulnerable, and the important realisation of its key role dawned on me when I watched the ground-breaking TED Talk by Brené Brown five years ago.

Many people will have seen this talk, which has received millions of views. (Here's the link: **http://bit.ly/2DAsflF/**). For those who haven't, I implore you to watch this wise, witty and wonderful 18-minute video and learn.

Brené Brown is proud to be a no-nonsense 'fifth generation Texan'. An academic, she describes herself as a 'qualitative researcher' covering social issues. When she was researching *connection* – she says that's 'why we're here; how we're wired' – she heard stories about disconnection and heartbreak from hundreds of the people she interviewed.

She concluded this was due to *shame* ("not being good enough or feeling worthy"), and, in turn, that "was underpinned by *vulnerability*". She reckoned that those people with a sense of worthiness had a strong sense of love and belonging – feeling "worthy of love and belonging". She concluded that these people:

- Were "wholehearted"
- Had the courage to be imperfect
- Were willing to let go of who they thought they should be to achieve connection
- Fully embraced vulnerability

Her mission in life previously, she said, had been to "control and predict" through research, but her connection survey had brought vulnerability into full focus, as the source of a wholehearted life – it was the exact opposite of control and predict.

"Am I alone in struggling with vulnerability?" she asks. "NO? ... We live in a vulnerable world, and one of the ways we deal with vulnerability is we numb it ... But I learnt from the research that you can't numb emotion ... (such as) hard feelings ... without numbing joy and gratitude..."

There's so much more in her talk – about children, about politics, about love, and about connection (about 'being enough'). I had become extremely adept at numbing my feelings. And, having watched this talk again and again, I'm still trying to take these lessons into my own life.

In her book *Daring Greatly*, Brené Brown writes: "The perception that vulnerability is weakness is the most widely accepted myth ... Vulnerability is the core of all emotions and feelings.

"To believe vulnerability is weakness is to believe feeling is weakness. To foreclose on our emotional life out of fear that the costs will be too high is to walk away from the very thing that gives purpose and meaning to living."

I have to admit that I have walked away and I have been standing back. I have tried to pluck up the courage, but I rarely managed to dare greatly.

If you have not watched Brené Brown's videos, or read her books, I commend them to you – wholeheartedly. If you have seen them already, watch again.

Emotional mastery

By the way, there's lots more great stuff to watch on TED.com and on YouTube. Another cracker is by psychologist Joan Rosenberg, who integrates neuroscience and psychotherapy in her talks on confidence, self-esteem, emotional strength, and resilience.

Vulnerability came into her TED talk on dealing with unpleasant feelings and achieving emotional mastery. It was one of the eight challenging or unpleasant feelings she listed. "I'm excited about unpleasant feelings," she said. "If you can experience and move through eight unpleasant feelings you can achieve anything in life."

The first step: "Make the choice to stay present, fully present. It's about awareness, not avoidance." She asked her audience whether, in challenging conversations they ran, hid, or got distracted? Or stayed present?

The second step: To "move through" any or all of the eight unpleasant and uncomfortable feelings as they arise. They are: sadness, anger, shame, helplessness, vulnerability, embarrassment, disappointment, and frustration.

"We are afraid that they will be too intense and that we will lose control," she said. "Our experience of emotional strength (in dealing with unpleasant feelings) is tied to our capacity to move through them."

Neuroscientists described emotions as a biochemical release, which flooded through the body to stir feelings and then went away, she explained. "What we feel emotionally is felt first in the body as a physical sensation. That's what we want to flee from or be distracted from – we don't want the bodily sensations."

The solution, she added, was to "ride the biochemical wave" which lasted 60 to 90 seconds. "Feelings are temporary. The waves come up spontaneously, and they will always subside."

A feeling like grief involved wave on wave, multiple waves, but they will always subside. When you think of a memory the same wave will be fired off.

"Surf the waves for 90 seconds and let them ride their course. Then insights will follow, and, with consistent practice, you will be able to unhook from your life stories (which are holding you back).

"What's holding you back? Stop and notice what you're feeling in the body. This is the path back to you being more fully you." https://www.youtube.com/watch?v=EKy19WzkPxE/

Dr Rosenberg's thesis – on waves of emotion, and the fear of losing control and being overwhelmed – certainly resonates with me. And I welcome her two-step process to manage unpleasant feelings.

34,000 emotions

The third TED talk, from 2015 in Oxford, I want to share was by the British neuroscientist Dr Alan Watkins on *Why you feel what you feel*. He started by outlining what we know of the progress of infant children, who have usually developed an awareness of their bodies by the age of 1, and an emotional awareness at about 2. Between the ages of 3 and 6, they become aware of the 'conceptual self', a conscious sense of ID. From 6 to 9 they develop a 'concrete consciousness', and they learn that there are 'rules'.

"That's where most people stay – emotionally aged 9 on the inside," declared Dr Watkins. During their teenage years, they are challenging the 'rules' in some way or another. Then, as adults, they learn to follow some (largely unknown) rules again to be 'good corporate citizens' – in a company and in society.

Later they question the rules again, if they have a mid-life crisis, which Dr Watkins calls a 'disease of meaning', when they are likely to adopt one or two strategies: Anaesthetic (alcohol or drugs); and Distraction (work, exercise and the gym, sex, or material things like shopping).

The meaning of life cannot be found in outside sources. "The problem is that the meaning is inside us. Emotions will determine our ability to make efficient decisions. Feeling is always there, but we don't always feel it."

Dr Watkins differentiates between emotions and feelings. Emotions are the energy which activates and motivates our feelings – compare this with Dr Rosenberg's waves of emotion where the biochemicals stream through us.

However, Dr Watkins upped the ante on his colleague by proclaiming there were potentially 34,000 emotions, which he compared to stars circling around planets in an emotional universe. He showed a graphic of this planetary system, which suggested to me there might be some semantics in his thirty-thousand-fold system, as some of the emotions had names which were barely distinguishable.

"If you don't know which planet and which galaxy you are in, you are lost," he said. Indeed I have felt emotionally lost for years.

Watkins' solution is to discover and navigate the emotional universe, with the help of an app which his company has developed. His emotional universe has positive and negative sides. Once you have located your spot, you look for positive planets.

"Imagine that all of us were from a planet where we wanted to be. If you can control your emotions, you will change your life completely."

https://www.youtube.com/watch?v=h-rRgpPbR5w&feature=youtu.be/

'Being brilliant every day'

So how is that achieved? We turn to an earlier TED talk in 2012 by Dr Watkins on achieving a positive mental state by controlling your thought processes. *Being brilliant every day* has had over 400,000 views.

The problem, he says, is that pressure and challenges create chaos which inhibits awareness and your ability to think straight. Thought depends on your biology and the context of a situation.

Dr Watkins adds: "We are designed that way. It's about survival. Your brain has to become unsophisticated and binary – fight or flight (or play dead). We have the same old software, and we haven't upgraded.

"As Einstein said: 'You can't solve problems with the same level of thinking'. How well you think at any time will depend on your biology. You have to change the context and the emotional state from which thoughts emerge. Then you can change the quality of the thought and the thought itself.

"Until we can take control of this physiology, anyone can make you look an idiot." The trick is to retain or regain conscious control of breathing through deep and rhythmic exercises.

This is slightly different from Yoga, which often encourages different breathing patterns and being aware of your breath. Deep and rhythmic breathing has to be smooth. It gives you 'coherence'. And you have to focus your attention on the heart and learn to regulate your emotions. The heart is the centre of emotions, Dr Watkins adds: "We say 'I love my son with all my heart' because that is where we feel it."

"The prime predictors of success are passion (which comes from the heart, as we know), determination and focus," says Dr Watkins. And he reminds us that athletes and coaches talk about a successful performer being "in the zone" or "in a state of flow".

A lot of Dr Watkins' premises make good sense to me. So hear what he has to say at: **https://www.youtube.com/watch?v=Q_ fFattg8N0/**

As I keep saying, I'm not an expert, but I find all these professional insights into human emotions and feelings extremely helpful.

Dr Alan Watkins

He is an Honorary Senior Lecturer in Neuroscience and Psychological Medicine at Imperial College, London and an Affiliate Professor of Leadership at the European School of Management, London. He originally qualified as a physician, has a first-class degree in psychology and a PhD in immunology. He is the founder and CEO of Complete Coherence and is recognised as an international expert on leadership and human performance.

http://www.complete coherence.com

Emotional intelligence

We know a great deal about IQ – Intelligence Quotient. It dates back to 1912 when it was mentioned in a book by the German psychologist William Stern. The score to measure intelligence is derived from specific tests, and many of them can be found online (e.g. at Mensa.org). IQ scores are used to assess people's capabilities in education and business, and for measuring disability. According to Wikipedia, approximately two-thirds of the population score between IQ 85 and IQ 115. About 2.5 per cent of the population scores above 130, and 2.5 per cent below 70.

To me, IQ has always seemed a rather arbitrary way of judging a person's personal attributes. Good for the measurement of intelligence, but there are many other factors which determine a human being's capabilities. The term Emotional Quotient (EQ) first saw the light of day in the 1960s, but it has become popular since the publication of Daniel Goleman's book *Emotional Intelligence – Why it can matter more than IQ,* more than 20 years ago. Before discussing Goleman, I will turn to Ush Dhanak to throw some light on the subject of EQ.

Ush wrote on her website (uskdhanak.com) in 2017:

"I define emotional intelligence as:

Being aware of your own emotions and how you handle those emotions; and then how you deal with the people you are with.

"Another important point about EQ is that, unlike IQ, it can be learnt. It's behavioural... As your emotional intelligence increases, so too will your personal power. Without it, you will be sacrificing your personal power and life will seem like a persistent knockback. In this negative state of mind, you will:

- Avoid confrontations
- Have difficulty speaking the truth
- Lack confidence in your judgment
- Avoid going to the heart of the issue
- Hesitate to try new things
- Have difficulty defending ideas
- Avoid challenges
- Give up easily
- Question your own ability
- Feel powerless
- Avoid risk-taking

This is the opposite of highly emotional intelligent people; the opposite of people who have personal power."

EQ makes sense

That sums up my own experience extremely well. For me, EQ makes sense. I have avoided confrontation and challenge. I do lack confidence in my own judgment. I have difficulty defending ideas; I question my ability, and I sometimes feel powerless. However, I do generally tell the truth (although I have occasionally been economical with it). I have taken risks, starting three new businesses during my life. And I don't tend to give up easily. Indeed my nearest and dearest have accused me of hanging on for too long when all hope is gone.

Goleman's goodies

In the Introduction, I cited Daniel Goleman, the author of *Emotional Intelligence* (EQ), and his views are worth looking at. He awards primary status to:

Anger

Sadness

Fear

Enjoyment

Love

Surprise

Disgust

Shame

He describes jealousy as a "variant of anger that also melds sadness and fear." And he admits that "there are no clear answers" on virtuous feelings such as faith, hope, courage and forgiveness, or "the classic vices, feelings such as doubt, complacency, sloth, and torpor – or fear / boredom".

Goleman wrote that 80% of success came from emotional intelligence (EQ) and only 20% from a person's IQ. He also said that EQ determines the success of a team or a group in a company. Humans have two minds – for thinking and feeling – and "the two sections of the brain operate independently".

Broadly, Goleman set out five EQ elements or emotional competencies:

1. Awareness.

2. Self-regulation – controlling your own destructive emotions.

3. Social skills – relationships.

4. Empathy – taking account of other people's feelings.

5. Motivation – the drive to achieve for the sake of it.

Goleman reckoned that emotional competencies could be learned, and also people could develop and change them. His model has been adapted since the publication of his book.

His views have been challenged by several academics, because, they have argued, EQ is not a form of intelligence but a form of behaviour, a skill rather than an intelligence. It muddles up well-established definitions of intelligence and could be used for manipulative purposes to undermine a person's rational thought processes.

However you categorise EQ, it adds a new dimension to the human condition from my point of view. Goleman, an American scientific journalist and trained psychologist, had his book published by Bantam Books in 1997, and it is full of facts and data, some of which are out of date, inevitably. In my view, it is well worth reading.

Aged 7, before leaving home

My emotional experience

Muddling IQ and EQ leads to what I shall call PIQUE. That is 'Personal Intelligence and the Question of Emotion'. My decision to try to control and stifle my emotions was an unconscious one. I can't remember taking the decision or even the lead up to it, or why I did it. After all, I was young – it was in probably the first 5-10 years of my life.

I have recorded some of my memories in the previous chapter, and most of them are recalled with joy. Yes, I also remember the shouts of anger and cries of pain as my parents fought mentally and physically in their bedroom near my nursery, as I have said. Can I remember what I was feeling? Was it fear, or pain, or devastation, or sadness?

As a child, my perception was that my parents were not happy together. I did not know why, and I did not understand what their fighting meant for me. I was not afraid of them or their fighting.

Did I feel afraid FOR them or OF them? I can't be sure, but I don't think I felt either – just perplexity. A sense of feelings might be too sophisticated for a toddler in a cot. Anyway, I did not feel insecure or fearful for myself.

In fact, in those early years, I did feel loved and safe. My home was all I knew, and I was content with it and in it. What more can a child need?

What emotional hiccup choked my sense of feeling and caused me to retreat from the wonderful world? It was almost certainly some occurrence, which may have been small and apparently insignificant, and which I have since buried.

I have done many role-plays in dozens of workshops in search of the event where I cut off my emotional progress.

Leaving home

With hindsight, the telling blow for me was being sent away to a private boarding school at the age of eight. Although I benefited hugely in academic terms from a private education, I'm convinced that my emotional and cultural development suffered.

There is a photo of me aged eight, standing in front of my mother's Standard 8 car at home about to set off for my first term at prep school with a big grin on my face. There I look happy enough. But at school, I felt lost and loveless for several weeks. I simply felt abandoned, and I will come to that in the Chapter on Learning.

The sound of rows

I feel real empathy for the late Emma Chambers, who played dippy Alice Tinker in the BBC comedy *The Vicar of Dibley* and died in February 2018 at the age of 53.

The Times obituary recorded that she was born into an upper middle-class Yorkshire family. Her father John was a consultant obstetrician and gynaecologist. Her mother Noelle was a pharmacist. The obituary goes on: "Her parents' marriage broke up when she was young, and Chambers would put her fingers in her ears to block out the sound of the rows." After an acrimonious divorce, her father emigrated to Australia, and she did not see him for many years.

"... (she) had an unhappy time at a very old-fashioned prep school," according to the obit. 'I was distraught at having left my mother, and it was the most horrendous place . . . I was so upset in the first week that one night I wet the bed, and I can remember taking the sheets to the matron and her screaming at me. It was the kind of place where they beat you.'

"She developed asthma and eczema and suffered from low self-esteem, a problem that never really went away... 'I don't like anything about my face,' she once said. 'I have a big nose, goofy teeth and not enough chin.'

"A much happier time came when she went to St Swithun's boarding school, Winchester, where she admitted she 'giggled a lot'. She played lacrosse to county standard and appeared in school plays, leading her on to formal training at the Webber Douglas Academy of Dramatic Art in London."

I hear echoes of Emma's experiences in my upbringing – the sound of rows, father 'emigrating' (though mine went to another home), an old-fashioned prep school, wetting the bed, beatings.

Rose Tremain is a favourite author, and *Rosie*, her memoir of her childhood and upbringing to the age of 18, was published in spring 2018. In the book she tells of a childhood with an absent father, a writer who abandoned the family when she was 10, when he went off with a younger woman, and a mother who was unable to love.

She and her sister Jo loved the Hampshire estate which belonged to their maternal grandparents. However, they had lost both their sons, killed in the war and by illness, and they just could not find a way to love Rosie and Jo's mother, who was sent away to boarding school at the age of six. Rosie was saved by her nanny, Nan, and an inspiring English teacher at her boarding school. Are you seeing any links here? Wheels within wheels. Circles within circles.

Mind, heart and spirit

These days we know far more about the influences of perception and interpretation, with the added spices of opinion and judgment. It is our perception, channelled through our minds, that plays fast and loose with our emotions.

As a young man, I came to believe (or believed all along) that my own opinion was worth much less than my ability to assemble facts and present a well-balanced argument. My feelings, such as they were, had even less importance in the great scheme of things, as far as my perception was concerned.

So I thought it best if my emotions didn't see the cold light of day. I lacked the courage to take the risk of being vulnerable and exposing my inner thoughts to others and to test them in front of an audience.

The English word courage is derived from the Latin 'cor' or heart, closely linked to the French 'coeur'. I was always lagging behind when it came to following Shakespeare's famous battle cry from *Henry V* to "stiffen the sinews and summon up the blood".

My perceived experiences of life have cast their shadow and contributed to an inability to find my feelings, to form intimate relationships and therefore to two failed marriages.

As I have said, in a number of workshops I have taken part in role-plays and also worked with various 'buddies' to help my understanding of my psyche. But these experiences did not encourage me to take hold of my courage and dare to venture into (what seemed like) the vulnerability vortex. In one memorable workshop – where a 'focus person' was chosen at random from cards with their names on, to go to the front and discuss issues and concerns affecting their lives – I was selected as the focus person five times out of six in one day. I still got no closer to solving my problems.

Practise saying what you feel

That's what I'm now trying to do. If only I had found the courage in the past to say what I felt. And I still find it difficult to express my feelings or to show vulnerability.

If asked the question, 'What advice would you give now to your younger self?' my answer would be: Have the courage to say out loud what you think and how you feel. Emotional vulnerability makes you more of a man or a woman.

I used to think that my thoughts and feelings could hurt other people. While the way you speak may cause hurt and offence, what you say is unlikely to be hurtful, especially if you are aiming to gauge a view; and, in the spirit of vulnerability, talking with openness and honesty and the willingness to be contradicted and challenged.

It's not what you say so much as how you say it. An open question is a much better approach than a bald statement. 'How do you feel when ...?' or 'What do you think of ...?'

Practice may not make people perfect, but it will give confidence and help along the road to development and growth. I know I've remained stuck in roughly the same place for far too long. Dr Watkins would say that I have found only nine emotions, and I am stuck in the under-nine age range.

Geraldine has described my silences as passive-aggressive and limiting the prospect of any good conversations between us. Silence is surely NOT golden.

Emotional prompts

I have learned to feel the emotions and monitor my feelings when an emotional balloon is pricked, and they bubble up. Emotional prompts include a song, a book or a film. They all help me to appreciate and understand emotions if I can just stay with them and dwell on them. The trick is to be aware of what you are feeling when a film or a book or a TV programme triggers your emotions. Here are some examples of my personal tear-jerkers...

Music: "Downloading emotions"

Songs, tunes, and lyrics have formed an important backdrop to my life. My musical taste is mainly pop, with a sprinkling of classical music. On 12 March 2018, I was in the car and turned on the radio. It was BBC Radio 2 and Ken Bruce's regular feature *Tracks of My Years* when famous names recall the musical milestones in their lives.

The feature had already started, and at first, I didn't recognise the speaker's voice, but he was talking eloquently about songs and music. He proclaimed: "Music, at its best, is downloading emotions – hearing what emotions feel like – at their core."

In fact, the celebrity was Ricky Gervais, who is not my favourite comedian – and I would probably have turned off the radio if I had known the speaker's identity from the start. Gervais' humour makes my lip curl, and I simply cannot listen to or watch his shows. However, his philosophy of music is completely in tune with mine.

My favourite music

My own top 10, to be whittled down to my 8 Desert Island Discs, are (right now, but my choices are subject to change):

1. *Smoke Gets in your Eyes*, The Platters
2. *Woman*, John Lennon
3. *Don't Give Up*, Peter Gabriel and Kate Bush
4. *The Living Years*, Mike and the Mechanics
5. *My Generation*, The Who
6. *Bridge over Troubled Water*, Simon and Garfunkel
7. *Is this Love?* Bob Marley
8. *Agnus Dei*, Fauré Requiem
9. *Adagietto* from Mahler's 5th Symphony
10. *Swan Lake*, Tchaikovsky (*The Dying Swan* and *The Finale*).

What, no Beatles? Stones? Dylan? Dusty Springfield? Annie Lennox (Sweet Dreams)? Bowie? No Mozart, Rachmaninov, or Beethoven? No music from the last 20 years?

These pieces of music strike a chord deep in my soul. For instance, *The Living Years* by Mike and the Mechanics always triggers tears. The song was written by Mike Rutherford and with lyrics by B A Robertson. Rutherford has said that "the song is about the lack of communication between B A Robertson and his father before his dad died."

The song won numerous awards and went to No 1 in the US, Canada, and Australia, and No 2 in the UK. Legendary songwriter Burt Bacharach has said that it was one of the best songs of the 80s and early 90s. The middle section of the lyrics goes:

I wasn't there that morning
When my Father passed away
I didn't get to tell him
All the things I had to say

I think I caught his spirit
Later that same year
I'm sure I heard his echo
In my baby's new born tears
I just wish I could have told him in the living years ...

In fact, I didn't become a father in the year my father died, but I did marry Susie. There are tears in my eyes as I write, as I hardly got to tell my father any of the things I had to say. But I have continued to 'catch his spirit' – later that same year, and in all the succeeding years.

Books with feeling

One of my favourite authors is the American thriller writer Walter Mosley. He has a special hero called Easy (Ezekiel) Rawlins, a black private detective who lives and works in the grey area between good and evil in Los Angeles, in the 1950s and beyond.

Mosley has a memorable way with words, characters and dialogue. The following extract comes from a recent Easy Rawlins novel *Rose Gold*.

Easy is talking about his girlfriend Bonnie from whom he is separated:

"I couldn't seem to get my emotions straight around her. I didn't love anyone else. I didn't want anyone else. But when we were together, I felt like a citizen of a defeated nation with no right to hold my head up."

That summed up my feelings when Geraldine and I separated last year and then finalised our divorce in 2018. But this was MY emotional response to our relationship.

A friend said: "How sad for you."

"Not sad for me," I replied. "It was my choice not to hold my head up. So that was sad for everyone around me."

Firm film favourites

Films and videos have always provided emotional triggers and moved me to tears. A classic cinematic example is provided by James Stewart as George Bailey in *It's a Wonderful Life*. This is one of my favourite films and always reduces me to tears long before the emotional climax.

George Bailey was a very good man who ran a mortgage company in the sleepy American town of Bedford Falls in the 1940s. He served his community faithfully – even depriving himself sometimes to help others. But, when things went wrong with his business (through no fault of his) one Christmas Eve, he lost faith in himself, and he wished he had never been born.

He felt isolated and worthless. So he decided to kill himself, stumbled up to the bridge over a nearby river, and jumped into the icy water expecting to die. However, an angel called Clarence had been sent to earth to save a soul (and earn his wings), and he jumped into the river after George to rescue him.

Then Clarence took George on a tour of an imaginary Bedford Falls where no George Bailey had existed, to show what would have happened to his family, his wife, and the inhabitants of the town if he had never been born. He was shown his true worth by how many lives he had changed and benefited. This made George appreciate his worth, and he ran home through the snow to his wife and family.

Frank Capra's film was a box office flop in 1946 but has since become one of the world's favourites, with a worldwide TV audience every Christmas. For me, this story is a lesson both in appreciating our self-worth and talking to people when things go wrong. George missed out on both counts, and I have been guilty of making the same mistakes, but I haven't tried to jump into an icy river in winter.

Another favourite film is *Good Will Hunting*, written by and starring Ben Affleck and Matt Damon. Will Hunting (Damon) is an undiscovered maths genius, who shows his hand to the world by unravelling a difficult problem written on a college board. Affleck plays his rather dumb friend – a good man with a poor brain. And Robin Williams gives a beautifully understated performance as the psychologist who helps Will escape from his demons. Another story of a man finding his true worth.

Inappropriate feelings

Finally, in this chapter, I come to inappropriate feelings, and what happens to them. I have found that, if I have bottled up my feelings, they can erupt at the wrong time in a burst of highly regrettable and offensive misogyny or racism.

Such inappropriate outbursts do not reflect how I think I feel about someone or some situation. But, somewhere inside, that sentiment must be churning round, unrealised and unresolved.

Me Too

Today we hear about inappropriate behaviour all the time. Recorded incidents start at the top, with Presidents of the United States, and work down through infamous abuses of celebrities like Harvey Weinstein and Jimmy Savile.

As I have said already, I have been accused of hating women. What if I really do hate women or disrespect gay people? I need to be constantly aware of my innermost feelings, as we all do.

To speak or not to speak? That has been the question for me all too often – and it has not been about hatred. I know it can take me a long time to process my feelings into rational thought and speech. So I end up not speaking, and that has been interpreted as not feeling, or passive aggression. I must be aware and hold myself accountable. Communication practice helps to soften and sanitise feelings.

Summary

I am still a long way from being able to access and express my feelings properly. I know that I have work to do. But I have the time and the will to become more readily aware of my feelings and to voice them.

I have tried building confidence in expressing my emotions and discussing them – in group activities, online and offline. Although these forums may be well moderated, I rarely have the courage to expose my vulnerable self to online groups who are largely unknown to me. You never know when you are going to tempt a troll to leap out and jump on your sensitive self.

I enjoyed some useful experiences at a men's group in Portsmouth run by two therapists, Jeff Lane and Simon Halford. In my experience, the discussions in a group of 8-12 men were usually worthwhile, eye-opening, male-oriented, and beneficial to the group. Sadly, the group disbanded – which may say something about men sustaining discussion of their feelings.

Emotions are parts of us all, and the subject is hard to summarise. They are always with us, and the challenge is to keep our hearts open, to stay vigilant and aware, to respect feelings when they come, but, after reflection, to send them on their way without letting them run (and ruin) our lives. Let vulnerability, wholeheartedness, and emotional intelligence be our guides.

In the next chapter, Think as well as feel.

Think as well as feel

"Our minds influence the key activity of the brain, which then influences everything; perception, cognition, thoughts and feelings, personal relationships – they're all a projection of you."

DEEPAK CHOPRA

This Much I Know

- Think as well as feel
- Feelings are complicated, but thoughts are manageable
- Hear the inner critic but move on and don't live by him/her

Complicated patterns envelop feelings and thoughts, and thoughts and feelings. They are interconnected. Our mental powers seem to release chemicals, which trigger our emotions so that unwanted feelings explode inside. Often the trigger means that our emotions overwhelm our thoughts and actions. Thoughts drive emotions, but feelings can control thoughts like back-seat drivers.

That is certainly true for me. In the last section, I discussed how a thoughtless emotion frequently could take control of me and disable my rational thinking process. I'm always telling myself to be aware of it and acknowledge it.

The Inner Critic

We all have an inner critic, telling us that we are not worthwhile; that no one will be interested in what we write, say, play or do. So our solution is to keep quiet and not bother anyone with thoughts, opinions, or performances.

I have been battling with that inner critic all the way through the process of writing this book – which has been both painfully difficult and exhilaratingly easy. When my inner critic pops his head up (the critic is definitely male), I now listen, acknowledge and let go.

In a workshop, author Julia Cameron (whose books include *The Artist's Way*) told her audience that her inner critic was called Nigel. Whatever the success of her books and talks, however appreciative her audiences, she still found that Nigel was appearing in her life, especially when she was writing.

Nigel always tells Julia Cameron how hopeless she is and that no one will pay any attention to her or buy her books (which, of course, they do in great numbers).

So she decided to take Nigel by the throat, or at least get a firm grip on his shoulder. Now whenever Nigel appears, she listens, nods her head and then says, "F*ck off, Nigel."

That reminded me of the 70s pop song, *Making Plans for Nigel*, written by Colin Moulding, bass player of XTC. This is how it starts:

"We're only making plans for Nigel
We only want what's best for him
We're only making plans for Nigel
Nigel just needs this helping hand

And if young Nigel says he's happy
He must be happy
He must be happy in his work..."

And it's true that our Nigels, those inner critics, receive far too much attention and respect. The negativity of a Nigel throws us off course and keeps us off our true path. We should want what's best for us, not for Nigel.

So the answer is to stay true to your rational thoughts, and to your heart, when you are drafting an article, a video script, a blog, a book, or a piece of music. That's one of the best lessons for me from the Book Midwife, Mindy Gibbins-Klein, who has guided me through the process of writing this book.

She instructed me to write the first draft quickly and assuredly, without looking back (or letting your inner critic get a look in). The time for careful consideration followed in the second draft, which was sent to my selected readers for feedback. Thank you, readers, for your invaluable contribution.

And, with the readers' advice in the background, I set out on the final draft – several drafts in some sections.

Spontaneity

This brings me to the subject of spontaneity because that was the guiding principle of my first draft. I don't know about you, but I often find that my best thoughts, talks and writing come when I'm not prepared, and I'm being spontaneous. These thoughts may well need some tweaking and improvement before they are ready for broadcasting, openly and adventurously.

And I find that my talks, or even elevator pitches at networking events, improve over time. The more I give the talks, and the more I write, the more fluent and easy speaking and writing become, and the process has not stopped. I find that, once I start talking or drafting quickly, the inner critic disappears completely.

It's strange how people lose the spontaneity of childhood before they grow up. As a very young child, I tended to be spontaneous and say what I felt. The inner critic comes with age, from five onwards, and is helped along by the outer critic provided by well-meaning adults in your circle of family and friends.

It may not be what they say but how they say it. This is where you encounter that 'it' moment when you begin to believe that you are inadequate, not worth it.

Positive thinking

There's another side to Nigel. That's positive thinking. Marianne Williamson has a famous quote on the subject: "Our deepest fear is not that we are inadequate. Our deepest fear is that we are powerful beyond measure. It is our light, not our darkness that most frightens us."

I have heard Marianne Williamson speak in London, and her talks always give me food for thought. She's on a par with Brené Brown.

I'm still fighting an intense battle with my inner critic, who prefers to tell me I am inadequate. But Marianne's words give comfort that there is another way.

Fortunately for me, positive thinking has come naturally, so it has always made sense and provided a powerful back-up. I have not found the need for the many books on positive thinking – such as, Norman Vincent Peale (*The Power of Positive Thinking*), Napoleon Hill (*Think and Grow Rich*), Dale Carnegie (*How to Win Friends and Influence People*). While our emotions are a powerful source of inspiration and creativity, they can also bring negative thoughts and body language.

Rational thinking

Some people use positive thinking to counteract the inner critic. But positive thinking may not always make sense, and that's when I prefer the notion of Rational Thinking.

As a journalist, I can write rationally about someone else, or about a topic which is dear to me. I was trained to write impersonally and objectively in the third person, never using the word 'I' if possible, and not letting my own voice or feelings intrude.

Articles are powerful if they are written with passion and commitment. But that works against the author if their words are not leavened with balance and reason.

As a trainee journalist in the 1970s, one of my jobs was to interview people who had just inherited money – following up wills printed in the local press. Surprisingly, people were only too happy to talk. I believe the experience was cathartic for them as they had access to a neutral, listening ear.

Strangely, I never used the interview/listening-ear technique in my private life. I used to believe that home and work were different, but I have come to realise that your true, authentic self will emerge naturally wherever you are, whether you like it or not.

So, if you are behaving differently at home, it is because your inner critic has got the better of your rational thinking. The two streams need to work together.

Negative thinking: depression

"Thoughts are the shadows of our feelings – always darker, emptier, simpler."

FRIEDRICH NIETZSCHE

The tangle of thought and emotion can precipitate many different states of negative thinking in people. And this can lead to depression, which afflicts many famous people, like Stephen Fry, Winston Churchill and others. Several friends have succumbed, and still succumb, to what some call the Black Dog. They seem as mystified as most of us by the causes of depression.

Of course, there are many different types of depression, with as many different causes. Is it an illness as some people have suggested?

Writer Matt Haig, himself an acute sufferer, has written many good books on the subject. He writes in *Reasons to Stay Alive*:

"Minds are unique... Depression looks different to everyone. If you have ever believed a depressive wants to be happy, you are wrong... They just want to feel an absence of pain."

For me, there have been downs but rarely the deep pain of depression. And I will hang on to Haig's 10 tips on 'How to be there for someone with depressive anxiety':

1. Know that you are needed.
2. Listen.
3. Never say, 'Pull yourself together'.

4.   Appreciate that it is an illness. Things will be said that aren't meant.

5.   Educate yourself.

6.   Don't take anything personally.

7.   Be patient.

8.   Meet them where they are.

9.   Relieve any work/life pressure if possible.

10. Don't make the depressive feel weirder than they already feel.

Bitten by the Black Dog

Even at the height of someone's success, the Black Dog can descend without warning. Recently, up-and-coming – but depressive – racehorse trainer Richard Woollacott was found dead only weeks after one of his biggest racing successes with his horse Beer Goggles.

"Richard Woollacott ... was found dead at his yard in Devon this week at the age of 40," was the bleak summary in *The Times*. "In her tribute, Mrs Woollacott referred to Richard's struggle against depression... with the lows, such as the loss of Edvardo (a horse), who was fatally injured at Wincanton on January 6, difficult to contend with."

His name and his fate reappeared at the 2018 Grand National meeting when Lalor, a horse now trained by his wife Kayley, won a major race at Aintree. Her pride and sadness were there for all to see. This was a powerful and tearful moment.

What makes me happy?

On the other side of depression street and its dark shadows lies happiness, bathed in sunlight. What is happiness – another elusive state of mind?

The first definition of 'happy' in the SOED is good fortune or good luck. And, more wordily, 'the state of pleasurable content of mind, which results from success or the attainment of what is considered good'.

- To see my family and friends at ease brings me a true state of contentment

- To live in a community which is generally contented, and which works together also makes me happy

- To be acknowledged for good work or a kind act

I had that community experience when working in Petersfield, in Hampshire, from 2006 to 2017. This was shown in the pages of the monthly community magazine *Life in Petersfield* which my company published.

We also inaugurated some awards to celebrate the happy successes of many types of artists, businesses, charities, eateries, clubs, performers, and teachers in the local community. I was overjoyed to see all the smiling faces at the annual awards event held at Petersfield Festival Hall. The awards have been maintained by the company which bought the magazine from us in 2013.

I am also happy when I have done a good job and been acknowledged for it. In recent years I have re-trained to Teach English as a Foreign Language. And I'm extremely proud of a testimonial from a London-based French intellectual property lawyer, Severine Mas:

"When you are a professional looking to improve your English, you need someone who understands business. Nick has given me the confidence to speak English, write business documents and interact with people in a confident professional manner. Nick is not just a tutor but a great coach! I would recommend him unfailingly."

It is also rewarding to receive thanks for volunteering work or for a kind act – although that is never why I volunteer or act altruistically. The question is: What makes you happy and how can you achieve it? I recommend helping others and being spontaneous for starters.

Hannah Power, the daughter of my good friend Penny Power OBE, summed this up beautifully when she told her mother, "You can't delegate your happiness to anyone. It is your responsibility and you have to fight for it and never give it up."

Happiness coaching

There are happiness coaches, such as Samantha & (aka Samantha Clarke), the founder of the Growth and Happiness School. Her aim is to 'elevate emotional intelligence' in companies and for individuals. She said, on the radio, she had a happy band of clients – some of them blue chip companies, such as American Express, Innocent, *Elle, The Guardian,* and the University of Cambridge.

You can find Samantha & on YouTube, where she says, "Ask yourself why you are standing in your own way of success..." THAT sentiment applies to many facets of our lives.

Hot off the press this spring comes new research from researchers at Oxford University in 28 countries where they found that our chances of being happy improve if we are better educated than our parents, especially men. Women were not affected in the same way as they are said to take account of factors outside their control when they assess their level of success or happiness.

And Julia Cameron says, "We don't always know what makes us happy. We know instead, what, we think, SHOULD. We are baffled and confused when our attempts at happiness fail... We are mute when it comes to naming accurately our own preferences, delights, gifts, talents."

The next chapter investigates issues around intimacy and sexual relations.

Relationships, love, sex and partnerships

"Intimacy seems to be one of the major highs in life, whether it's getting to know yourself in a deeper way, or your partner, or the world and the society you live in."

JEFF BRIDGES

What I've Learnt

- A good relationship is the key to intimacy
- There is a big difference between intimacy and sex
- Find intimacy and deep affection by respecting and appreciating your partner and yourself

Power of good relationships

The title of this chapter omits the all-important word 'relationships'. Without a proper relationship, you cannot achieve any satisfactory love, sex, intimacy, marriage or partnership.

That searing truth has been brought home to me through two failed marriages. And the two missing parts of my relationships, which go hand in hand, were communication and intimacy. You may think I'm repeating myself, but I feel that I can't say this often enough.

When my first wife Susie told me she was leaving me, I can remember the scene as clearly as if it were yesterday. We were standing in our sitting room, and I asked her if she loved me at all. She raised her hand and whipped it sharply under my chin in a scything movement – to indicate that it was my head not my heart which appealed to her.

My second marriage to Geraldine was more than twice as long as my first – it lasted, or rather endured, for 30 years. Geraldine has said that I came out of the marriage much the same man as when I went into it, and I would agree with that summary.

I was constantly and rightly accused of non-communication and passive aggression. I had not learned the power of love but was gripped by the power of fear, which left me powerless to express my feelings. This lack of courage was my failure, and I regret it bitterly. I can only apologise wholeheartedly for my fearful and self-centred silences. The costs of this cowardice, for Susie, Geraldine and me, were: lack of intimacy, absence of empathy, and the ruin of our relationships. Of course, it takes two to make or break any relationship, but I certainly played a starring role in these two long (and almost certainly too long) melodramas.

Where did things go wrong? It goes back to my (mis) perceptions of women from an early age. For a start, I completely misunderstood my mother. She appeared to me, in my child's eyes, as over the top and insensitive to other people's feelings for much of the time, especially in public and after a couple of drinks.

However, many years later at that painting therapy workshop, I depicted her with an unhappy face and tears rolling down her cheeks, as I have written. That image has created a lasting impression which keeps coming back to me.

Mixed feelings

I have been accused of hating women and avoiding intimacy. My belief is that I fear both women and intimacy. Although I grew up in a household of women – Mum, Nanny and later Granny Keith – they were from another generation; and I always felt nervous of females my own age, starting at children's parties. I did not know what to make of them. I recall at the age of six being petrified when I was paired for a dance with a pretty, dark-haired girl in a long white dress.

Women remained a mystery when I met the sisters of school friends. I was afraid to be touched by them, let alone dare to touch them if I found them attractive. When one girl, the friend of a friend, put her hand firmly on mine while we were watching TV, I pulled rapidly away. It was foolish and fearful adolescence. I wanted things to happen, but I did not know how to behave or how to communicate. Instead of showing how I felt inside, I held back, held fast and held on to my fears.

The sexual revolution in the 1960s largely passed me by. Even at Oxford I was living in fear of women of my age, enjoying their company without ever putting myself forward in any way. I was a beta male. I was not pleased with or proud of this stifling inhibition.

Dream sequence

So, for a number of reasons, some of them incomprehensible, I have never felt comfortable or confident with women. This was summed up for me in a vivid dream I had in January 2018.
The dream went like this:

I was at a station about to catch a train to London from the up platform. A snacks wagon had pulled up at the end of the down platform. I thought I just had time to buy a drink before my up train arrived on the opposite platform. But my train arrived just as I reached the front of the queue. In scrabbling for change I dropped all my money and, by the time I had recovered it, my train was on its way. I shrugged and looked for my bag which I'd put on the floor. It had gone. Stolen, I believed.

As I prepared to wait for the next train, my wife Geraldine arrived, and we agreed to travel up to town together. However, when the train did arrive, she strode ahead and found a seat where there were no free spaces either next to her or opposite.

So I went to the next carriage, which was formatted like a small boat with a circular bench in the middle and seats around the outside (all occupied). An attractive woman was performing stretches and exercises on and around the bench.

I kept observing her from the corner of my eye while pretending to read a book. When I looked up from my book, I saw she had stripped to the waist and was posturing provocatively.

No one else seemed to be interested or watching. She was like Tina Turner's *Private Dancer*. I was embarrassed and did not know what to make of it. Eventually, she stopped exercising and sat down at my feet, resting her back against my legs.

I didn't know what to do. Was she flirting, or should I sit still and ignore her provocations? I sat in a nervous silence, wondering whether to stroke her hair but not daring to move. The dream ended there.

Reflections on a dream

In life, I have remained prone to embarrassment, blushing and unsure of myself or how to behave, and puzzled by women. This was neatly exemplified in the dream: What to make of Geraldine not sticking to her agreement in the dream to sit with me on the train, and the unknown flirt with her comely cavorting?

Why did I not challenge Geraldine in the dream for not sitting with me as agreed? Why did I feel powerless, impotent even, in the face of the dancer? Not daring to move has been my standard procedure in dealing with unfamiliar women from a young age right to my mature years.

There was little help from the media which was always banging on about the 'Swinging Sixties'. There were films like *Alfie* (which starred a young Michael Caine) and *The Knack,* but they seemed to focus more on exploitation of and disdain for women. That was not at all how I felt about them. Anyway, I never discovered the real knack – openness and vulnerability.

Inside intimacy

Achieving intimacy is essential to enduring relationships, but it is not all about sex. Far from it.

"There are a thousand different definitions of intimacy," John Karter writes, "and most of them concern the qualities of openness, honesty and vulnerability, and the willingness to share our deepest fears, desires and other feelings with our partner."

Dr Harriet Lerner adds (from *The Dance of Intimacy*) that an intimate relationship is "one in which neither party silences, sacrifices or betrays the self, and each party expresses strength and vulnerability, weakness and competence in a balanced way." Notice 'vulnerability' popping up again.

So far almost all these qualities and skills have been beyond me. They have eluded me in both my marriages and largely in my relationships with my four children. Let's hope that it's never too late to learn and acquire new emotional skills so that I can achieve emotional expertise.

Transform your sex life

My friend Simon Halford has long worked as a psychologist, specialising in psycho-sexual therapy for more than 20 years. He practises in Harley Street and also in the South (where he lives). We met more than 10 years ago when he was facilitating the men's group with his colleague Jeff Lane.

In 2006 Simon and I worked together on a book to help *transform your sex life and relationship*. Simon provided the expert information and the case studies, while my job was to write the text, edit and publish the book. My first big mistake was to insist on calling it *Intelligent Sex*, which I thought was a catchy and clever title. But it is too clever for its own good because the title misleads. Sex is instinctive, spontaneous, and emotive (rather than 'intelligent').

Simon wrote in the book: "Quality sex means different things to different people at different times. One of the most important qualities of healthy sex is integrity of purpose. In healthy long-term relationships good sex characteristically happens between people who talk in some depth about their wishes and dreams, likes and dislikes."

He put 'fulfilling sex' in three categories:

1) Physical, psychological and relational.

2) The importance of context: time, place, well-being, safety and confidence.

3) The four stages of sexual activity: desire, arousal, orgasm, resolution.

"If all these aspects are broadly working together, that will ensure good sex," he concluded. "My belief is that the warning light should go on for couples who are having sex fewer times than once a fortnight. Frequency isn't everything ... But you need to take stock if the average gap is more than two weeks.

"If you aren't enjoying one of the most pleasurable human experiences more often, why not? What is wrong, not just with your sex life, but with your relationship and your lifestyle priorities?" Part 1 of *Intelligent Sex* is about managing your sex life: Defining and maintaining fulfilling sex.

Sex is a many-splendoured thing

Tom and Polly, a vibrant and creative couple in their 30s, enjoyed a good sex life in the early years of their relationship. They talked about everything and had similar appetites for sex. They lived together for seven years before marrying.

Polly's libido declined after the birth of a son. "After the baby our sex was OK, but it never got back to what it had been before," said Polly, who had also undergone surgery and experienced difficulty conceiving their second child.

Through conversation, Simon established that their sex life had declined for three reasons. They both worked hard – Tom in TV production and Polly as a home-based editor and proofreader. Polly had health issues after surgery. And there was a mismatch because Polly felt she was having sex to get pregnant, not for her own sake or for him. Her unconscious negative messages and Tom's desire not to press his needs on his wife meant that they had stopped having sex.

So a strategy was agreed to improve her libido and reduce the mismatch by reintroducing integrity of purpose for their sex – "good healthy sex has to be sex for sex's sake" – on the advice of Simon.

Part 2 of *Intelligent Sex* concerns problems: relationships; having children; men's and women's physical problems; loss of libido; mismatch in needs and expectations; scripts and 'inflexible beliefs'; issues around obsessive behaviour, work, drugs, alcohol; and finally health, illnesses, transmitted sexual diseases, and contraception.

At the start of Part 2, Simon returns to the power of relationships. "Relational problems often underlie the sexual difficulties that couples present... People tend to resist a relational problem. Generally, couples are loathe to hear that they need to do something about their relationship as well (as a sexual problem)."

Communicating needs

A professional couple in their 50s, Peter and Anna, had stopped having sex. He feared erectile dysfunction, while she felt unloved and unwanted. As a result, she was frustrated, sad and suffered from loss of libido. They said that sex had gradually declined over the years and stopped completely with a bereavement after the death of a grandchild.

Simon Halford commented: "They had failed to prioritise sex or communicate their needs to each other. They had simply defined themselves as a couple too busy to have sex."

In the clinic with Simon, they mapped the decline and cessation of sex and agreed a strategy to reintroduce it into their lives. This strategy meant:

1) Communicating and openly discussing their needs.

2) Prioritising sex (even putting in their diaries) and having the right context.

3) Adapting their lives to help points 1 and 2.

"And that was exactly how they proceeded to restore healthy sex. They talked about what they liked and disliked. The first stage involved being affectionate and having quality time together. Sex was taken off the agenda to remove any fear or frustration.

"They learned to get to know each other again with meals out and text messages, or trips to the cinema. They learned how to pleasure each other without having penetrative sex. They made steady progress, and they were restored to sexual health. Anna felt loved and appreciated, while Peter realised that he could be a successful sexual partner without penetration.

"A high-quality sexual relationship came through clear communication... A genuine success story reviving a relationship which had been allowed to wither through neglect with no ill-intent on either side."

Needless to say, I failed to heed the wisdom in Simon Halford's book. I remained living in my head, not my heart, and that's probably why I wanted to call the book *Intelligent Sex*. After all, intelligence is not only about the brain, but it is also about gathering and using information.

Sex addiction

On the other side of the coin is sex addiction, the opposite of intimacy, which is just as destructive to love, intimacy, and contentment as anything. This has been highlighted by the publication of Erica Garza's book *Getting Off: One Woman's Journey through Sex and Porn Addiction* – excerpted in *The Sunday Times*.

There is nothing happy or fulfilling about her sad story, which has yet to be resolved in her 30s. "At 30 years old, at 24, even at 12 it was impossible for me to think about sexual pleasure without feeling shame," she writes, admitting that she discovered the meaning of orgasm at the age of 12, started using sex chatrooms on her computer at 13, and lost her virginity at 17.

"In my mid-twenties I turned to a new venture – casual sex … Enjoyment isn't a big enough word to describe what I got from these casual encounters. It was a mixture of shame and excitement that I had come to depend on."

After that, she says, her sex addiction ruined one relationship after another. As she approached her 30s, she realised she had no self-worth – she didn't love or respect herself. So she went on a retreat in Bali and did "yoga, reiki, met other travellers"; and there were "Sex and Love Anonymous meetings in the basement of a church."

The excerpt concludes: "I wish I could tell you… that I'm cured… I'm not going to wait until I'm some pure and perfect person to consider my journey valuable enough to share. That person… still has cravings… but what she doesn't have is the desire to stay stuck."

In my life, I have experienced few intimate relationships, but that is largely the result of my emotional shortcomings.

Chapter 6 explores what really drives people – money, work, intimacy – or something else?

Decide what really drives you

"Money won't make success;
the freedom to make it will."

NELSON MANDELA

This Much I Know

- Discover what really drives you
- Find a job which is fun, whether you work for yourself or for others
- Courage, persistence, energy, and resilience at work are positive
- Learn from mistakes; be prepared to fail – and fail falling forward
- Avoid being a slave to work and money

What really drives you?

The road to discovering what truly drives us can be long and winding. Lucky are those who have work-life balance with a fulfilling home life and a job which they enjoy. The big question is: how do we feel about our home lives and our working lives, our friends and our business colleagues!

Sometimes there seem to be so many opportunities and so much enjoyment at home and at work. At other times, the struggle seems unequal, as shown by the sad story of racehorse trainer Richard Woollacott.

There are many potential sources for feeling fulfilled, and we are driven by many different thoughts and emotions at various stages of our lives. But I believe we need to be aware of our drivers. The prime motivators are family, work, money, and sense of worth – but not necessarily in that order.

Money, money, money

"Money makes the world go round, the world go round, the world go round. It makes the world go round... Of that, we can be sure."

The words of this famous song from the 1966 musical *Cabaret* are hard to forget. The context of the song is important. Christopher Isherwood's story is set in 1930s Berlin as the Nazis are steadily gaining power. The setting is a sleazy club, and the memorable song is delivered by the Master of Ceremonies (played in the 1972 film by Joel Grey).

Personally, I have always been somewhat *laissez-faire* about money. I reckon this attitude was gleaned from watching my father. He was cavalier about money; he never seemed to have cash on him for, say, a train ticket, and often had to borrow from my mother.

For me, the moral of the song *Money* is that wealth can lead to corruption, distress, deception and downright misery. Happy are those whose attitude to money is considered and respectful.

Entrepreneur Luke Johnson, chairman of Risk Capital Partners, wrote in his column in *The Sunday Times* on 22

April: "To build a company you need to compete in the market. It involves voluntary exchange and free will. By contrast most transactions with the state concern coercion.

"Business is a wonderful route to expressing practical creativity. By achieving successful product and service innovations, the private sector has an impact on millions of people every day – it makes a positive difference."

From my point of view, you need to work as much for fun as for money. If you enjoy your job and you work smart (rather than hard), you are likely to be better at it. But watch for the trap of becoming a workaholic. I have always worked hard (but not necessarily smart!) and enjoyed my jobs. Indeed I have usually felt in the right place at the right time. If you are not enjoying your job, it's time to think again. There are plenty of opportunities.

Too much money

And if you have too much money? Abundance treated with consideration and respect brings satisfaction. And you can always help others. My own sense of wealth has not come from money, but from giving of myself, in jobs, in communities, in networks and in volunteering – though not, of course, in my private life.

I know several high achievers personally who get their satisfaction by investing in businesses, crafts or other projects, without any anticipation of necessarily getting a return. They are hoping, of course, that their business acumen will bring rewards to the people they support, or the enterprises or charities will prosper. Bill and Melinda Gates, for example, are repatriating their wealth to good causes, such as health care.

Too little money

Scarcity brings its own set of challenges. It is fascinating to see how people meet those challenges, avoid them, or fall and fail. Lack of money is bound to make people feel insecure, anxious, and worthless. The idea that, if and when people fail, they are 'failing forward' appeals to me. This is the typical business attitude from the United States; Americans have a different idea of the outcome of failure from the British.

For instance, Thomas Edison did 1,000 experiments before he successfully produced a light bulb. "I have not failed, I have just found 1,000 ways that didn't work," he said. And James Dyson went through 1,200 development processes before he perfected his bagless vacuum cleaner.

The ideal salary

A study of 2,000 British people in 2015 (commissioned by Anchor Cheddar) showed that their ideal salary was £34,000 a year. And in the US, a survey in 2016 by David Clingingsmith, at the Department of Economics, Case Western Reserve University, found that the ideal annual salary was around $80,000.

The more people earned above $80,000, the less effect it had on improving their satisfaction levels. "Above $80,000, the effect of percentage changes declines, reaching zero at $200,000." In 2015, the average annual wage in the US was $55,000.

The authors concluded "that high income buys life satisfaction but not happiness. Health, care, giving, loneliness, and smoking are relatively stronger predictors of daily emotions."

That sums up how I have always felt about income. I have been lucky enough to have lived in an age when property ownership has provided a bedrock of capital and financial security to some people. Moving home, or downsizing, have given a financial boost to wealth. In addition, I have had the benefit of a bequest or two.

My life's work

Alongside my family in my married life, my work has driven me. I have enjoyed the vast majority of my jobs. From the age of 21 to date I have worked in the communications industry, and, as I have said, I have loved almost all of my work experiences. That, I believe, is rare.

After graduating from Oxford and deciding to train as a journalist, it took me the best part of a year before I could find a newspaper publishing house to employ me. Eventually, in spring 1969 I started on a three-year training course (known as indentures) in a local weekly newspaper, the *Watford Post* part of the Luton-based Home Counties Group.

In those days the first job of a junior reporter was to walk round to the local police, fire and ambulance stations to check whether there had been any incidents in the night to follow up. Other tasks included reporting on cases in the magistrate's and county courts, covering parish and district councils, attending shows, fairs and local events.

As a trainee I was taken to watch the print processes: to see how the edited copy and page layouts (done by more senior staff) were sent to the printers; and the paper was 'put to bed'.

As I liked sport, I volunteered to report Sunday football matches in Watford and help the sports editor, Graham Collier, compile round-ups on other sports. In 1970, Watford reached the semi-final of the FA Cup, beating Arsenal and Liverpool at home at Vicarage Road. Their opponents were Chelsea, and I was sent by Graham to interview the manager Dave Sexton for the *Post's* semi-final supplement – at the time Susie and I lived in a flat off the Fulham Road, a short walk from the Chelsea ground at Stamford Bridge.

When I arrived for my appointment, there was a larger-than-life *Sun* football hack in Sexton's office. Much to my delight, Sexton told him to "Clear off while I talk to a decent member of the Press." Anyway, the semi-final had no fairy-tale ending, as Watford lost 5-0 at White Hart Lane.

The days of the *Watford Post* were also numbered. Not long afterwards the paper was closed by Home Counties because the competition from the other local papers was too strong. I was steered towards completing my 'indentures' (training) at another local paper, the (Luton) *Evening Post*, based in Hemel Hempstead with its sister the (Watford) *Evening Echo*. The *Post* was a slick, modern, professionally run paper owned by Lord Thomson, the Canadian publisher who was a quiet powerhouse in the British media in the days of the Beaverbrooks and the Rothermeres, and before the advent of Murdoch.

At the *Evening Post,* I found my journalistic metier in features. This included a well-received series about people to be affected by the proposed building of a third London airport in Buckinghamshire; and a day with the local MP, Shirley Williams.

A feature by me on Shirley Williams in 1971

Based in the paper's Hitchin office, one of my colleagues was John Blake who has since found fame and fortune as a publisher in biography and non-fiction. John Blake Books list more than 600 titles on their website. Another was Bill Wigmore, who used to drive to Fleet Street in the evening to do shift-work on the tabloids. When I clocked into the Hitchin office at 8.30am, Wigmore was often to be found asleep on the floor after a London shift. I was impressed. Here were two young journalists who seemed to me to be at the sharp end of the newspaper business.

Cuckoo

The golden years of my journalistic career were at *The Times* from 1972 to 1982 (including three as Sports Editor). I started as a graduate entrant on the Letters Page.

There used to be a myth that one of the regular letters in *The Times* was from the reader who heard 'The First Cuckoo'. However, no such letter appeared in the two years I worked on the letters page.

In 1972 when I joined *The Times*, their offices were at Printing House Square by Blackfriars Bridge. Text was transported from the sub-editors to the printers via an old-fashioned system of wires and pulleys. The tour of the building for newcomers focused attention on a corner of the ceiling of a small loo where copy regularly was dislodged from the line.

After a year, *The Times* moved offices to Gray's Inn Road to a building renamed New Printing House Square. The Letters department had three journalists and two secretaries. We sifted through the 300 letters to the editor each day – both to complain and to be published – and acted as the Editor's communications/PR department. Letters of complaint were shown to the Editor and other relevant people for action or a recommended reply.

Most letters for publication were sent to a specialist to get a view of their worth, or shown directly to the Editor, who had the final choice of the lead letters. Contrary to popular belief, the main criterion for publication was whether a letter made an interesting point, started a discussion or contributed to an existing thread.

We tried to publish expert letters and those from readers without a handle to their name. MPs did not have privileged access to the Letters pages unless they were making a useful contribution. One night I had a vivid discussion with Caroline Benn, Tony's wife, as to why her husband's letter had not been published. It did not add to the debate.

Another notable event during my working day when I was occasionally deputed by the Letters Editor, Geoffrey Woolley, to attend the afternoon editorial conference at 4pm. Then each department head announced their likely main news story, feature, letter or sports item to their colleagues and the Editor, William Rees-Mogg (father of Jacob). In those days most people's sporting interests at *The Times* were limited to cricket and rugby.

My life felt very civilised and special. With the vetting of letters, I became acquainted with a wide range of expert correspondents on the paper. I also learned to write a good letter, although 90 per cent of the replies were standardised.

However, after two years on Letters, I was ready to move on. My dream was to become a foreign correspondent, but there were absolutely no openings. So I settled for a place on the Sports desk as a sub-editor. That was great fun, as I loved sport. But the hours became increasingly anti-social. Shifts started at 2pm, 3pm and 5pm, and ended 7 or 8 hours later. Those were the days when newspapers were printed using hot metal, and the unions were firmly in charge of the print processes.

On the Letters page, I had some experience of working on the 'stone', with the 'compositors' or rather 'stone hands' or 'comps', the print people that sub-editors had to deal with. The stone was where the metal galleys of type were arranged in the desired order and prepared for print. (Other compositors were typesetters, who had already set the text into its metal format, but I had no dealings with them).

Managing the Letters pages on the stone was a leisurely process, as the deadline for Letters was early, and the layout of the page was formatted and simple. Sport proved a different challenge. The sports pages were usually allocated two or three broadsheet pages. In those days, *The Times* did not take seriously its sports content.

On Sport, we had a great team of people. There was constant banter, lots of jokes and laughter. We worked towards the first edition deadline at 7.30pm, with later editions for 10.30pm and a final edition at midnight. The layout and content of the pages varied from one edition to another to accommodate developing news and sports stories.

The first edition pages had to be ready ('off the stone') by about 9pm. The second edition went to bed at 10.30pm, so there was an almighty scramble when there were a lot of midweek football matches (especially on European Cup nights). The games finished at 9.30pm so there was only one hour to sub-edit and set the text and manage it on the stone.

Some of the 'comps' loved sport and were very cooperative in working skilfully through this frantic process. Others were surly and sluggish. At weekends I was lucky enough to be sent to report matches. I started with soccer but soon moved to rugby union. Our rugby correspondent in those days was Peter West, famed for his work on TV, mainly BBC (rugby and *Come Dancing*, the forerunner to *Strictly*).

I soon moved up the reporting ladder and was given the secondary international fixture on Five Nations' weekends. This meant memorable visits to Murrayfield (Edinburgh), Cardiff Arms Park, the Parc des Princes (Paris), and Lansdowne Road (Dublin) to cover the home games of Scotland, Wales, France and Ireland.

The most fun were the encounters of the Celts involving Ireland, Scotland and Wales. My favourite ground was Lansdowne Road, Dublin, for an Ireland v Scotland game. On one occasion, I was invited into the room of a group of Scottish medics who were drinking gin at 10am. "For heaven's sake, don't report this in *The Times*," they joked.

Paris was another remarkable venue for its sights and smells. On the way to the game, inside the ground, you saw live cockerels and fireworks, smelt the whiff of garlic, and witnessed wine gushing from wineskins.

During my life at *The Times*, we endured the miserable and unmemorable year when the paper was closed because of an unresolved confrontation between the printers and the management. The CEO was Duke (Marmaduke) Hussey, who seemed distant from his staff and ran a management team that was not widely respected in-house or in the wider world. But the problem of the rogue print unions was huge, although it was soon to be solved by Rupert Murdoch, who had taken over *The Sun*, and was eventually to own *The Times* and *The Sunday Times* (our more successful sister who kept us afloat for years).

During our year out, most of us went to work regularly on a part-time basis, and from time to time prepared dummy editions, printed in Germany... just in case. After the dispute with the printers and the stoppage ended, the Sports Editor John Hennessy retired, and I was selected to take his place at the age of 32. A proud moment.

While life was never dull as Sports Editor, you have to remember that I was a manager looking after the staff and the sports pages. So most of my work was office-bound. I did manage to get away to favourite events or venues, such as the Open golf, all the major cricket grounds and horse racing tracks, and football stadia like Anfield and Old Trafford.

By this time Murdoch had bought the Times Newspapers Group from Lord Thomson, and Harry Evans had moved over from *The Sunday Times* to take charge as Editor of *The Times*. These were good days for me as Evans was interested in sport and introduced me to using graphic illustrations on the sports pages.

When Ian Botham scored one of his centuries in the famous 1981 Ashes series against the Australians, I returned to my office after a boozy lunch with a friend to find Harry jumping up and down. He was wondering where I was at three o'clock in the afternoon, and ready to quiz me about how we would present Botham's epic batsmanship in the paper the next morning.

I made a few phone calls and found a freelance to create a graphic of Botham's innings – showing in what area of the pitch he scored his runs; and which were 1s, 2s, 3s, 4s and 6s. These types of diagrams are now widely seen in newspapers and on TV.

Evans truly brought *The Times'* journalists and editors up to scratch. For instance, on the night of an assassination attempt on President Reagan, he insisted on seven editions of the paper, the last at 3am. However, he brought in several outsiders to form a 'kitchen Cabinet', crossed swords with many of his senior staff, and he had a running battle with the owner.

When Evans came under pressure from Murdoch, and his position was clearly threatened, his cronies went around the senior staff seeking signatures to a petition supporting him. By this time I was an Assistant Editor, and I reckon that I was just about the only person in a senior position who had worked on *The Times* before Evans' arrival to sign in his favour. I thought that his drive, knowledge and newspaper skills were good for us all. I never heard the result of that poll, but very soon Harry Evans had resigned.

I felt that it was time for me to move on. Indeed I was sure that the anti-social hours were taking a toll on my marriage and family life. Furthermore, *The Times'* management told me that they saw my future in sport and that there was little likelihood that I would find the equivalent opening in another department.

My preview as Sports Editor on the main feature page of
The Times of the 1982 World Cup in Spain, won by Italy.
Above it, a piece by Enoch Powell questions the UK's
relationship with the UN, at the time of the
Falklands War with Argentina.

So I took an opportunity to set up a publishing business to produce 10 guide books about watching sport on TV (the *Sportviewers' Guides*, for David & Charles). I decided that I could not do justice to my role as Sports Editor while managing the writing, editing and print of these 10 books. So I resigned in spring 1982 with a six-month notice period. I wanted to be the Sports Editor for the football World Cup that year.

Entrepreneurial escapades

When I handed in my resignation to John Grant, the Managing Editor of *The Times*, I gave him the reasons outlined above. When he asked if there was another, personal reason, I fibbed and said I just wanted a change.

The trouble was that my marriage to Susie was in trouble – and the trouble was far worse than I knew.

To make matters worse for me, Roger was my partner in the new venture, and he had introduced me to David & Charles. He was in the print business with lots of publishing contacts, and his role was to find out what they needed, brainstorm ideas for books with me, and introduce me to potential clients.

While I was still at *The Times*, we created and produced a guide to the 1982 World Cup for Rainbird, a paperback which was distributed in supermarkets, like Safeway. In September 1982, I left *The Times*. In spite of everything, my new company Siron successfully produced a series of books for two years as contract publishers – selling ideas for books and producing them under contract for publishing firms which undertook the sales and marketing.

For David & Charles, we created the 10 *Sportsviewers' Guides* (e.g. Athletics, Darts, Golf, Snooker, Rugby League, and Wrestling), and a biography of Torvill and Dean, who had just won ice skating gold at the 1980 winter Olympics. And for the publishers Hamlyn we commissioned and edited *1000 Best Movies on Video* – video was relatively new in those days.

I was proud of all those books, especially *The Sportsviewers' Guide to Golf*, which I wrote myself. The best sellers were Darts and Snooker! However, after two years I found the pace of producing books painfully slow, and the grind of an awkward relationship with Roger somewhat painful. It was time to move on.

For the next five years, I worked in the magazine sector of publishing. Reed had just acquired a small publishing company which was having huge success with a free magazine called *London Portrait*. The publication made a good profit by selling London property ads, which filled the first 100 or so pages of the monthly magazine.

The owners convinced Reed that they had a scheme for a free title which would achieve the long-awaited breakthrough into the men's magazine market (this was before *GQ* etc.). I was hired as Editor of *London Gentleman*. When that failed after a year, I remained in the group as Editorial Director of *London Portrait* and *London Living* (formerly called *Property & Investment*). In addition, we launched customer magazines for Shell (1 million copies of *Freewheel* distributed at petrol stations), Jaguar Cars, and Britannia Airways.

In my mind, I was ready to become an entrepreneur again, this time as 'a publishing agent' – producing magazines, brochures and newsletters for corporates to help them communicate either with their clients or staff. I thought my new business could offer a nimbler and even more customer-focused service than a large traditional publisher like Reed, where such magazines were an afterthought.

For a year I went freelance for a large publishing agency where I worked on a desk producing supplements for *TIME* magazine.

I wrote the text and an American woman 'translated' it into *TIME* speak. To get up to speed with modern technology of electronic printing, I did Saturday shifts on *The Sunday Times* sports desk, specialising in processing reports by Stephen Jones, who is still their rugby correspondent.

This introduced me to desktop publishing (on a large scale). Long gone were old-style print and printers – hot metal, compositors and the stone. They had been replaced by digital methods, whereby copy and pictures for newspapers were edited and designed into print-ready format by journalists using the new technology.

So in late 1989, I was ready to start. My new company was called Blackfriar Publications, named because I used to meet my co-founder Bob Cook in a pub near Blackfriars Bridge. We hired a graphic designer, Jonathan Smyth, bought two Apple computers (already the computer of choice for designers), and rented a small office near Hanover Square, London.

The business had much stronger foundations, with capital investment from shareholders. They were university friends and business acquaintances of mine and Jeremy Dawkins, an Oxford accountant friend. It was a tricky first year, and the work did not provide enough revenue to employ three people. We had to part company with Bob at the end of the year because his business leads were not bringing in enough work.

In January 1990, one year on, we were thinking of folding the venture when a lucky lead brought us a huge client. Eastern Electricity was the biggest utility company after the government's reorganisation and privatisation of the electricity sector. We worked with Eastern for seven years, producing two customer magazines, *Power for Business* and *Power for Property*. We also produced publications for the following companies under contract:

- International Olympic Committee (marketing bulletin)
- Knight Frank (staff magazine)
- Rolls-Royce Motor Cars (staff magazine)
- Sky Sports *(2 Ashes* cricket magazines)
- Yardleys of London (staff magazine)

In addition, I re-launched *Sports Quarterly* magazine for Third Man publications, which was great fun, and took me back to my roots. However, like all good things, it had to come to an end. I could see the end coming for Blackfriar when large publishing companies like Condé Nast and Nat Mags realised the potential of contract publications, which they had initially dismissed.

Blackfriar was squeezed between the rock of major publishing houses and the hard place of large contract publishing businesses, such as John Brown Publishing – now called **John Brown Media**, which claims to be "world leaders in content marketing. We've mastered the art of crafting positive conversations for the world's best-loved brands and have been since 1987."

Well, Blackfriar was only three years younger than John Brown, but it had to be put back in its box and was quietly wound up. After Blackfriar, I reverted to working as an editor and writer, providing editorial services through my company Keith News Ltd ("If a personal name is good enough for Ford, it's right for you," I was told by my half-brother Patrick Barbour, founder and chairman of Barbour Index, a publicly listed company).

In 2006 I joined Navigate, a marketing company, to help launch two community magazines, *Life in Petersfield* and *Life in Haslemere*, and I later became the Communications Director and shareholder. In 2013 Navigate was sold. So I retrained as a TEFL teacher. More of that experience in Chapter 7.

Modern work life

The 21st century methods of communication – emails, Facebook, Instagram, LinkedIn, Twitter, WhatsApp, texting and so on – have provided me with interesting and enjoyable challenges. I know many people my age hate them, but there's a potentially exciting world out there in cyberspace for silver surfers like us. We just have to take care.

Online, you need the same skills and awareness as when you live and work in a big city:

- Keep your eyes open
- Take care where you put your trust
- Beware of what seems like a good thing. If it's too good to be true, it's almost certainly a scam. So be suspicious

So, I have always tried to achieve balance in my jobs. That's when work works best. All work and no play makes no sense at all for this boy. So my lifetime habit was to take a break for lunch and leave my desk. When I had to take work home, I made a great effort to do it before any of the family had got up. I've always been an early riser! The old adage is to work smart rather than work hard. That surely means: taking breaks during the day; spending plenty of time at home with your family and friends; making maximum use of your leisure time; and trying to leave your work behind at the office.

Of course being at home, as a housewife or househusband, counts as full-time work. Indeed looking after children and a home are just as difficult and stressful as going to work – if not more so. How often is work-life balance achieved, especially for people in their 30s, 40s, and 50s?

In your 30s, you are probably climbing the ladder.

In your 40s, you are trying to maximise your earnings at the peak period of your working life, while at the same time fighting off the challenges from younger people.

In your 50s, you are looking over your shoulder even more, knowing that it will be hard to get a job if you are made redundant.

Money and work are not the most important things

In spite of the fact that I have enjoyed my working life, I have always known that the job was not the most important thing – even if I may not have honoured that precept in my married lives. Indeed work-life balance has become ever more difficult to achieve.

One of the most striking factors of modern life is that most of us are working much longer hours, taking work home, and working at weekends. And this fact has two striking side effects:

1) We are suffering stress and worse health, so

2) We become ill more often, miss work and even burn out.

We are not working any smarter or more efficiently. This is one of the perils of modern living. Earlier generations, such as my baby boomer group, are working comfortably later into their lives because they have trained into this cycle of work. I'm not saying that they necessarily work any smarter, but they have got physically and mentally fit for today's work style by a gradual introduction.

Now people expect to start their working life at full tilt with no steady build-up of pace. If you are an athlete, it's like trying to run a marathon at the pace of a 1,500 metre runner. It can't be done.

This is all part of the widespread belief that, if people don't get on the career ladder immediately, they will be swamped by the next year's group of graduates. Today working life can be a treadmill. But it doesn't have to be.

People now in their 30s to 60s are envious of the earnings of younger people and feel obliged to copy their work rate just to keep up, keep a job and keep earning.

Some of this is down to the urge to earn as much money as young as possible. In the City of London and some big legal firms, some graduates are earning £30,000 a year as soon as they start work. "The current average graduate salary in the UK is just shy of £23,000, but we've also heard folk reporting everything between £16,000 and £70,000," according to Savethestudent.org

In May 2016, Denmark was named as the top European destination for graduate salaries, in a *Daily Telegraph* report of a survey by Transfer Wise, the money transfer platform. Denmark came top because its cost of living is lower than in second-place Switzerland, where starter graduate salaries are close to 100,000 Euros. The next three countries in the study were Sweden, Germany and Norway.

In other European countries, graduates do not enter the workplace until they are in their mid-20s, four or five years older than in the UK where people get a job as soon as they leave university at 21 and 22.

Family dynamics

Family relationships are important drivers. But, as you grow older, and through adulthood, the relationships with your parents, siblings and close relations change. The question is whether family becomes a brake on your career or a stimulus for your personal growth and development. Or, more probably, work becomes a brake on family life. Besides, parents and family may bring pressure to succeed, especially if the work is in a family firm. A spouse and close relations may put on the pressure to earn more money, or work more, or stop being lazy – or all three.

Personal

Three factors are often quoted as the key elements of success and fulfilment: health, wealth and time. We have to consider our own attitudes to work and money – among many other things. At job interviews or in workshops people are often asked: 'In an ideal world, if you had a magic wand, what would you like to do and what would you like to earn?'

In 2017 a friend's son went for a job interview, was offered the job, and was asked to go back to the company the next day with a decision on whether he wanted to accept and how much he wanted to earn. That was an almost impossible task. He took advice overnight from family and business friends. He took the job and asked for a salary which was £1,000 more a month than he was earning. His submission was accepted without question.

He has wondered since whether he should have asked for more money. But he concluded that:

1) He did not feel the job was worth more;

2) He did not think he was worth the extra money; and

3) He would have felt under pressure to perform if he had asked for, and got, more.

Here are issues surrounding moral codes, accountability and satisfaction. His moral code told him that the value of the job was not higher than the money he requested; responsibility told him he was worth a certain sum of money, not more; and the accountability to the company and himself told him that there would be extra pressure on him with an 'excessive' salary – and that would have put pressure on his performance and therefore would be against everyone's best interests.

Social

What happens away from the workplace with your friends and relations – including leisure, hobbies, sport, the arts and travel – needs to be where you find the fun to help fulfil your dreams. Socialising with friends, family life, and entertainment – television, radio, theatre, ballet, sport, exercise and books – are all part of this area.

Events in your city, town or neighbourhood – fairs, festivals, food, drink, and carnivals – provide great scope for getting together with others, meeting people, communicating, and finding your niche in local society. Witness the two community magazines which I have launched in the last 12 years and mentioned above.

Spiritual

As the power of religion recedes in some places, we seek answers to matters of the spirit and the soul issues. There is a lot of choice and a large library of books on spiritual matters. I have taken an interest in wider spiritual work, as my Church of England Christianity has waned; and I believe it is important to try different options. Only late in life have I started to examine comparative religions and philosophies. Having visited many mosques in Istanbul, I have found them holy, simple and spiritual places of worship – **See Adventures, page 181.**

Company pressures

Back to the commercial world, pressures in businesses and organisations tend to build up when things are not going well. Sales are stagnant or falling; profits are down; management is poor; conflict and disharmony are rife; competition is increasing; working conditions are declining. All this means there are layoffs, redundancies and promises from management which are known to be unreasonable or even false. So staff are asked to take pay cuts (temporary) and/or work longer hours and do extra jobs.

I appreciate that this is one side of the story. And many businesses have succeeded by operating from the opposite standpoint. I have witnessed and experienced the big challenges of business life in my career – starting with the closure of the *Watford Post* and the tribulations of *The Times* in the 1970s and continuing with my own intermittent problems running businesses in the 1980s, 1990s and 2000s.

With the wisdom of hindsight, I regret that I was not always more open and communicative in business. Good leadership, good management (of people and finances), good communication, and good relationships epitomise best business practice.

"What's at the root of business problems?"

Maybe, I would have benefited in my working life if I had heard a TED talk with this title by David Emerald. He said:

"The masculine is the structures and systems that provide the safe home for the business to be in – so websites, business plans, marketing plans would come into that too.

"The feminine is the nurturing and connection – so customer service, networking, the connection side of marketing and also making sure that the business nurtures your own goals and needs as well as those of your customers.

"The child aspect is the creativity, openness to new ideas, exploration of ideas, the enjoyment of the business and the ability to get back up again after you fall like children learning to walk do. The child is also the holder of the bigger vision for the business."

While drafting this book I was directed to this talk by a blog from Jacqui McGinn who had been reading The Power of TED: http://jacquimcginn. com/whats-at-the-root-of-business-problems/

Incidentally, your father is said to be the inspiration for your business life. My father was the child in

> this process. He had the creative vision but NOT the "structures and systems that provide the safe home..." neither at work nor in my home life.

Cultural pressures

The western world lives and works in a capitalist culture. Those in favour of capitalism say the markets are the best way to provide for a well-endowed society. Antagonists argue that capitalism favours those with money and does not provide for a fair society.

Those in the middle (many of us, I suspect) want the best of both worlds: to have a society which is well provided for, but fairly. The media fans the arguments. As the press is predominantly conservative (not always with a small 'c'), the pressure to support money and capitalism is ratcheted up, especially at election time.

Peer pressures

There is also the human pressure, which comes from envy. Whenever I read or hear about someone who works in my field of expertise and realise that they earn far more than I ever did, I can't help feeling envious. I would say that is natural, and I must add that the envy does not last very long. Envy is one of the watchwords of the inner critic: you need to acknowledge it is present, dwell with it awhile and then send it on its way.

People at work, and at play, can be highly competitive. So we all get peer pressure from our colleagues at work, our friends and neighbours. Even our family can add to the pressure to make money, either directly or by inference, sometimes subtly sustained.

All we can do is live with the pressure if it is there, acknowledge it and talk about it. There's no point hiding in a cave when the pressures are on. I know that I have not done enough to discuss and challenge when under pressure.

I have tended to keep quiet and hope the pressure and criticism will go away or change. But it tends to lurk in the background, half-hidden but never dispelled, preventing me from getting on with my job (in every sense of the phrase). When I have felt pressure, I have failed to communicate it too often.

Material pressures

Shortage of money brings pressure on your home and your mortgage, on your wish to live in a better house, own a better car, go on more exotic holidays, and have smarter possessions. I have felt and experienced all these scarcities. It's hard to make the best of what you have got. But it's possible, and the need to do so ties in with living with vulnerability and communication – talking to everyone putting on the pressure, including yourself.

Sex

Finally, is sex your driver? How balanced is your sex drive? But, just as with every other element in the system, good communication with your partner is absolutely vital. This has not been a major driver for me, though my unwillingness to communicate has affected my sex life. However, I empathise with the character in the Ray Davies song *Lola*: I can truthfully say that "I'm not the world's most physical guy, but I know what I am. I'm a man. I'm a man...."

In the next chapter, Learning and the impact of education on people's personality and spirit go under the microscope.

Education: School, university, training and personal development

*"The beautiful thing about learning is
nobody can take it away from you."*

B B KING

What I've Learnt

- Boarding school blunted me and many others emotionally, even those who did not suffer physical and mental abuse

- The culture of boarding schools is unlikely to provide pupils with a rounded education, emotionally and academically

- Mental and physical abuse remain serious in the boarding school system

The parental conflicts at home did not interrupt my own learning progress at school. I felt OK about myself academically. While I was shy, like a lot of people, I made friends and seemed at peace with my world. I enjoyed a privileged private education and did well at school. The emotional doubts started when I was sent away to boarding school from the age of 8, as happened to many middle-class baby boomers.

In the very early years, before the age of five, I can remember three junior schools with joy and affection. My first experience of school was with Miss Puck's nursery at Puttenham where we lived. Then, when I was aged five, for one term I attended a play school where the teacher memorably arranged the chairs like an airplane (probably she called it an aeroplane) to teach us geography.

From six to eight, there was the Marist Convent near Ascot, where the nuns used to hand out Merit Badges to worthy students, including swats like me.

At boarding school from 8 to 18, I was removed from family life for 36 weeks of the year. My mother often complained that I always seemed to be at home, but that was not my experience! Boarding school did take me away from the hothouse of a chaotic home life, but my homes always felt warm and comfortable.

While I can't say for sure when or why my communication channels started to close, this was almost certainly hastened by being sent away to boarding school in September 1955. Before I went to Horris Hill, I was blissfully unaware of any clouds on my horizon. Then the clouds and storms rushed into my life.

I remember spending many days standing at the back door of the school crying my eyes out. And I started wetting my bed – a sure sign that I was deeply unhappy. My grandfather Leo died during my first term at prep school, and that upset me too.

All these things combined to throw me off my emotional balance. Slowly I pulled myself together, however, and unwittingly put my mind to points 2 and 5 of Goleman's EQ model – self-regulation of my emotions; and motivation (achievement for achievement's sake). My life turned around, and I learned to make the most of the world of the boarding school.

Fortunately for me, I did not suffer abuse at school, nor did I witness any of the appalling physical and mental abuses inflicted on children at some boarding schools. And this bullying and violence was also prevalent in girls' schools.

However, after the initial shock, boarding school was largely a joy for me between the ages of 8 and 18. I 'boarded up my life' in a new sphere where I set myself to be silent, strong and stalwart. I settled into school life and enjoyed success. I felt fulfilled at school but was that fulfilment at the expense of my emotional development? I had no siblings to rub up against and perhaps they would have provided some insights through observation and example of someone with close blood ties.

I wouldn't have dreamt of mentioning any of the feelings I had to my family, to teachers or my school friends. While I might be sorry for a friend who was unhappy, I felt powerless to say anything to help or do anything about it.

That, for sure, has remained true for most of my life.

So what about the millions of men and women who were day pupils at state school? What may have held them back from showing vulnerability and learning emotional intelligence?

The British character tends towards reserve and stoicism. Sayings such as 'Big boys don't cry' and 'You're a brave girl for not crying' are widespread in all walks of life. The social, economic and political primacy masculine values have long stunted the feeling realm, and therefore the spiritual growth of the people who have ruled, and still rule the UK.

Blunted by boarding school

So it's now become clear to me: my emotional development was blunted by boarding school. Later in life, I used to comfort myself that it saved me from the slings and arrows of my parents' stormy relationship. In one sense, boarding school was a blessing in disguise, I reasoned privately. But boarding school life persuaded me unconsciously to suppress any sense of openness and adventure.

Of course, these were my feelings and comparisons are dangerous. When I hear stories of other people's childhood experiences, they seem more deprived and make mine seem somehow unworthy. For example, Kriss Akabusi, the British Olympic gold medal winning athlete, has told how he was put in a foster home when he was age 4. He recalls, "I cried for my mother until I was 12. Then I realised that I was never going to see her again."

Dawning of reality

Looking back over more than 60 years, I acknowledge that my muddled, childish perceptions were a mixed blessing and they tricked me into concealing my emotions. This is no plea for sympathy but a dawning of reality.

In 1955, private education at a boarding school was the only way to go for the vast majority of middle-class parents with money. They paid good money to get their children a good education, in good schools, where there were good facilities and a good network of friends and acquaintances for their kids to meet.

Private fee-paying boarding schools continue to do an excellent job teaching their privileged attendees academic excellence, and training them how to get into university and then to get on in the world. They also contribute to a warped class system in British society, which favours money and rank, and hinders our national development. This is because emotional development and intelligence have to be achieved in spite of the educational system, and not because of it or with its help. While I'm proud of my academic achievements, I'm dismayed and ashamed of my emotional failures.

In no small part these emotional failures have contributed to two failed marriages and an under-par performance as a parent. "Oh, he doesn't say what he thinks or feels," I have heard it said of me.

I believe we would all have better and stronger family lives if it weren't for boarding schools, which are totally irrational if you think about it. And, in another life, I would choose to send my children to day schools. In many ways, I wish I had not gone to boarding school, but that was out of my control.

A divided and divisive school system

That is for the future. The educational past is deeply rooted in an academically divided and socially divisive school system. Sixty years ago money and class were the watchwords of parents. Today the key factors are money and brains. Class is no longer enough unless a boy or girl can pass the entrance exams. The educational system in the UK remains skewed in favour of that elite. The survival of the class system is a blot on British society and a hindrance to our progress.

While we are not all created equal, it is wrong that inequality of opportunity begins at birth and is cranked up when children go to fee-paying schools, where classes are smaller, and facilities are often better. Why, I have often wondered, has no government had the courage to remove the charitable status from the public schools so that they and state schools have a more level financial situation?

The case for abolishing private education

I reckon that the UK would be greatly improved as a nation if private education was abolished. Of course, there would be inequalities in the levels and standards of education, as some schools would be better than others. But we would have a better, fairer and more united society if the educational system was more level and less divided. And this country seems more divided than ever before.

Alan Bennett summed it up for me in an interview, "I do believe that if private education was abolished, and we only had one system of education, the whole atmosphere of this country would alter. A lot of the class divisions and silly stuff about old Etonians in the cabinet, all that would go. I just feel that we would be much more a nation."

That prospect seems as remote today as ever. I don't accept the argument that it would be against human rights to deprive rich people of the opportunity to give their children a better financed education. Surely education is a human right, and that is flouted if an unfair advantage derives from income.

David Kynaston, an Oxford historian and an abolitionist, has said, "Endless reports point to the privately educated stranglehold and the sheer disparity in life chances."

The annual cost of educating a student at a state school outside London is equivalent to roughly half a term's fees at a top private school. And I have read that "Serious attempts to claw back anomalous tax advantages from the independent sector have usually ended in failure. In 2011, the courts in effect returned to private schools the right to decide what constitutes 'public benefit' in return for charitable status." This was according to Melissa Benn, in an article in *The Guardian*, in May 2016.

https://www.theguardian.com/education/2016/may/31/private-education-must-go-westminster-school-melissa-benn

Abuse in boarding schools

There is also the vexed question of abuse of children in boarding schools, boys and girls. The abuse of boys in private boarding schools has been brought into sharp focus by journalist and broadcaster Alex Renton.

Old Etonian Renton experienced abuse himself at his prep school, Ashdown House. He has interviewed hundreds of other people to reveal that perversion has been widespread and insidious, particularly in private boarding schools.

He revealed the ugly truth in his book *Stiff Upper Lip: secrets, crimes and the schooling of a ruling class;* and in the ITV documentary *Boarding Schools: The Secret Shame* in February 2018; and in newspaper articles and social media.

"This *(Stiff Upper Lip)* is the story of generations of parents, Britain's richest and grandest, who believed that being miserable at school was necessary to make a good and successful citizen," Alex Renton declares on his website. "Childish suffering was a price they accepted for the preservation of their class and their entitlement. The children who were moulded by this misery and abuse went on – as they still do – to run Britain's public institutions and private companies."

There are horrific stories in the book and in the documentary. The most frightening discovery is that adults, teachers and parents, colluded with the abusers, mainly to protect the reputation of the schools. Several of the abusers were the head teachers. And one convicted paedophile teacher blamed the boys for 'leading him on', suggesting that, at the age of 11 they wanted a sexual experience.

At the two private boarding schools I attended, I witnessed none of this. And, I was assured at a recent reunion of Horris Hill old boys, that people may not have experienced abuse, but they had felt the fear of it. One former pupil, younger than me, made the shocking statement that abuse, and perverse practices were part and parcel of boarding school life; and the threat of them taught people to look after themselves. He said he knew Renton and thought that the stories and effects of abuse were being overblown.

But, if you imagine that abuse in boarding schools is a thing of the past, that is not necessarily the case. Renton stated in his Twitter feed on 7 March 2018: "Abuse of children in institutions won't end – because the government decided yesterday to stick with a child protection law that's far weaker than in much of the rest of the world." @axrenton.

Indeed, bullying and psychological abuse are a damaging aspect of boarding school life, which Renton's 'ruling class' seems to accept complacently. Often they send their children to boarding school even though they hated it. The stiff upper lip approach to life does not encourage the open, courageous and vulnerable young spirits who can truly prosper in adulthood. They are forced to conform to the rigid rules and narrow academic testing which Sir Ken Robinson deplores (see below).

And there is the added concern, expressed by Renton and others, that privately educated pupils have their emotions squashed at boarding schools – even if they are not physically or mentally abused.

For me, it would be prudent to reconstitute private schools completely:

- Remove their charitable status
- Keep their positive values
- Upgrade schools generally, under the control of those directly responsible for education (not government ministers or civil servants)
- Provide the choice to board for children with special needs of various kinds

Focus on UK education

Abolishing or downgrading private education would be a big step. Another course of action – more achievable, but still difficult – would be returning education into the hands of the professionals with responsibility for it, so it is no longer run by politicians and the civil service. For best results, the management of the education system must be put in the hands of the women and men who have deep and long-term experience and knowledge of it.

Politicians and civil servants have tinkered with and messed up the educational system for far too long. They have no grounded experience of educational management; all new education ministers want to put their stamp on the job, and ministers change jobs often, so there is little room for continuity, even within each political party, let alone among the main parties.

In the December 2016 Pisa (Programme for International Student Assessment) rankings, the UK was a middle-of-the-table performer in 15th place – behind countries such as Estonia, Finland, Vietnam, Canada (7th), and New Zealand, Slovenia, and Australia (12th, 13th and 14th).

The top five countries for reading, maths and science were:

1. Singapore
2. Japan
3. Estonia
4. Taiwan
5. Finland

In science, the UK was ranked 15/70; in reading, 22/70; and in Maths, 27/70 following tests that were carried out on students aged 15. In the UK there is an outcry every summer, after the publication of exam results in schools, colleges and universities. Commentators complain that modern exams are too undemanding. Business states that far too few students have the right educational qualifications in their special subjects or lack the soft learning skills (in teamwork and communication).

Yet the centrally controlled curriculum fails to provide many of the learning topics required. For instance, Sir James Dyson has founded an institute in Bath to train engineers, but there are only 100 places.

Let creativity inspire

No one who has watched the TED Talks of the English educationalist Sir Ken Robinson (or read his books) will doubt that the outcomes for students, and therefore for the country's future and for people's creative processes, are being handicapped by educational systems, and not just in the UK.

There have been more than 50 million views of Sir Ken's TED talk in 2006 on how to have a nurturing education system which builds creativity: **https://www.ted.com/talks/ken_robinson_says_schools_kill_creativity**

And in another TED talk in 2013, he offered three principles crucial for the human mind to flourish – and how current education culture works against them. The three principles are: to offer variety, not conformity; to stimulate curiosity, 'the engine of achievement'; and to create creativity in and the possibility for both students and teachers.

Humans are 'naturally different or diverse', but education is based on conformity, he says. Science and maths are important, but they are not sufficient. "A real education has to give equal weight to the arts, the humanities and physical education.

"Kids prosper best with a broad curriculum that celebrates their various talents, not just a small range of them. And by the way, the arts aren't just important because they improve math scores. They're important because they speak to parts of children's beings which are otherwise untouched."

He said that Finland performed well in international education tests partly because these tests focused solely on science, maths and English. But Finland's success was mainly because it encourages openness, diversity and creativity in its educational processes, which have very little standardised testing.

https://www.ted.com/talks/ken_robinson_how_to_ escape_education_s_death_valley

Teaching students hand skills

As well as diversity and creativity, another missing link in the education system is the teaching of hand skills, sometimes thought of as 'creative' skills. Peter Mucci, a fellow of the Royal Society of Arts, Manufacturing & Commerce (RSA) says, "The majority of products, from computers to aircraft carriers, are made, maintained or repaired by hand, by technically able and qualified people. This requires high levels of creativity and intellectual skills at pre-production, production and post-production stages."

But many people have these skills naturally and can improve them to 'high levels' with training. He adds, however, that workshops and labs are disappearing fast from colleges and universities and being replaced by computers. The new army of robots and Artificial Intelligence (AI) aids will not replace the 'craft' skill of trained humans to make accurate judgments in precise 'hands-on' activities, he says.

Peter Mucci and two other fellows of the RSA, who all come from an engineering background, have launched a major initiative to boost the manufacturing industry in the south of the UK, through creativity and innovation. And I have started working with their newly formed organisation, Hands on the Future (HOTF). This sets out to:

- Create hands-on skills experiences
- Support apprenticeships
- Raise the profile of the manufacturing industry

They deplore the "mistaken belief that products are cheaper and better when sourced from abroad; and the myth that craft skills exclude intellectual ability." They add that there is "an almost total lack of industrial experience, education or training among MPs, and a public service mindset against private manufacturing companies."

An award-winning mechanical engineer, Peter Mucci has been a manager, inventor, university lecturer, and joint external examiner with James Dyson to the Royal College of Art (RCA) master's degree in industrial design. He deplores the blind faith of academics and politicians in the idea that the UK must become a 'knowledge-based society'.

"Hand skills are almost completely excluded from the list of recognised qualifications for degree courses," he says. "Surgeons are exceptions to the low regard given by society to those working with their hands. However, more lives are at stake in the hands of aircraft engineers."

I'm happy to be working with HOTF, helping them with the marketing and communication efforts, in their bid to get their vision more widely recognised. Their hope is that, if they can spread the importance of hand skills and training in southern England, this could foster a wider movement.

"The happiest days of my life"?

Now, it's back to the future to tell you about my school life in the 1950s and 1960s, and what I've learnt. After the initial shock and horror of being dumped in a boarding school, I learned to close my emotional hatches and fit into the culturally and academically monastic regime. In the life of both my boarding schools, I played a full part: I was head boy at my prep school and head of house at Eton. I worked hard and enjoyed games (although I was not very good at them), made friends and kept a low profile socially.

In those days, Horris Hill had a reputation for academic and physical austerity. It prepared boys for the Winchester Entrance exam, academically harder than Common Entrance. The regime was strict and structured, with cold baths every morning before getting dressed and having breakfast.

I thrived in a regime where I neither experienced or witnessed abuse or bullying by masters or boys. Indeed the only sexual abuse I encountered was from a godfather, who was a fiddler of boys even though he was married with two children. But his fiddling did not cause me any long-term damage. However, many fellow students told me later that they suffered from the regime, were bullied, and missed home dreadfully. (Nevertheless, years later some still sent their sons to Horris Hill!) I was an academic success and worked hard to get into the 1st XI football team at left back. In those days the school was very good at football and we hardly ever lost during the five years I was there.

For the record, my nickname from the masters was 'Rowdy'. The communication clue is in the ironic nickname because I was

NOT a typically noisy or open young man. But I was sociable and had lots of friends, as I have said. The exeats (a single day away from school) happened three times a term on a Sunday after church – no overnight stay, and no half-term. On my exeats, I would take 2 or 3 boys home to Herons Brook, where we always had a cracking Sunday lunch.

On some Sundays, I went to a friend's home. One of them was called Philip Beck, whose father was headmaster of Cheam (where Prince Charles became a pupil). One of our after-lunch recreations was to have a conker fight with the Cheam boys, including the Prince. And I swear I once hit him a glancing blow with a conker. Treasonable boy!

Life at Eton

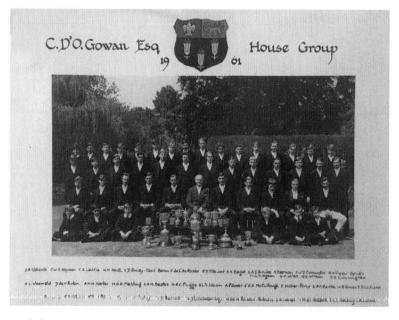

I did well in Common Entrance in the summer of 1960 and won a good place at Eton College, which was much less academic in those days. Indeed I had been so well taught at prep school that I could easily have taken O Levels (GCE) at the age of 14. But that was not permitted in the system unless you were an exceptional scholar. So I was coasting and a bit bored with work in my first three years.

At Eton, with my own bedroom from the start, I learned confidence and resilience – and developed a harder shell and an even greater tendency to keep myself to myself. I certainly learned to be even more guarded and reserved than I had been in the past.

Friends during my teenage years continued to play important roles. I did not have as many friends as at prep school, and they were mainly confined to my house. The school roll was more than 1,000 students divided into houses, so there was a good mixture of people to choose from as friends in your house.

College, where the scholars boarded, was itself a house.

My closest friends at Eton were Hal Bagot, James Showers, and Robert Gayner. James was a man of country sports, mainly shooting and fishing. Hal was the charming son of a landed family with a grand property called Levens Hall, which was in the Lake District near Kendal. James and I spent many a happy outdoor summer holiday with Hal in Cumbria (or Westmorland as it was in those days), fishing, frolicking, and water-skiing on the lakes.

We spent one summer staying in a shepherd's hut, swimming in tarns and trying to catch fish. The River Kent which flowed through the grounds of Levens was where I caught my first fish, a bonny sea trout. I can still remember terrified journeys back to the big house from night-time fishing expeditions in Levens Park where a dripping tap sounded like footsteps or the rustle of leaves stirred up devilish sensations, which scared us so much that we always broke into a dash for home.

We were old enough to have lunch with the adults. I still feel shame for showing up my two pals by being quick-witted at mental arithmetic and constantly displaying my prowess at the lunch table.

Robert ('Bertie' as he is now known) and I became friends in our last two years when we were in the same class for German. When I could drive at 17, I spent many hours in my mother's car going to visit him at his family home, which was in the Oxfordshire village where *Chitty Chitty Bang Bang* was filmed.

What was Eton like? In my first year, there was a spate of bullying in the form of 'debagging' when two or more boys would enter your room and pull your trousers down. This was an unpleasant ritual to establish power rather than sexual. After the bullying episode was discovered and punished, life returned to normal.

Eton suffers from a huge mistaken mystique. It is widely misconceived as being a hothouse for snobbery and elitism – and certainly, you meet Old Etonians who match the standard caricature of the arrogant, snobbish, chinless wonder, complete with silver spoon. However, students in my day came from a wide variety of family backgrounds and varied in temperament and outlook.

Many OEs, like me, have kept quiet about their educational background because it leads to misunderstandings about who you are. Of course, I have made maximum use of the benefits of the education and the OE network. But in some professions, it was a disadvantage to flaunt the old school tie – journalism was one of those. I was much readier to promote my university education, as that was acquired entirely on merit and not bought – at a time when university education was still free.

University entrance

When I won a place at Hertford College, Oxford, in 1965 to read modern history, I was as surprised as anyone. This was against the run of play in my exam trials and therefore against all expectations including mine. However, I was very good at exams, working fast and well under the pressure of the three-hour exam clock. This was one of the reasons that I decided to train as a journalist.

I can still remember opening the small, white envelope postmarked 'Oxford' in my study at home before Christmas 1964 and seeing that I had been offered a place. I could hardly believe my eyes, and that my hard work had paid off. This was the proudest moment of my life so far, apart from when I won my football colours at Horris Hill.

I had developed no plan of what to do if I had failed to get into Oxford, nor did I have any thought of attending another university. Neither had I considered working or travelling in the gap period before going to university in October 1965. So I was allowed to stay on at Eton for another two terms. A waste of money perhaps, and a missed opportunity for me to have a gap period, working and travelling for experience.

However, I was made captain of house for those last two terms, so I had experience of sorts managing people and teams. With a new housemaster in place, there was work to do, so I felt I benefited from my time. One of the hidden highlights was escaping from the house one night and walking across the River Thames to a club in Windsor where the Yardbirds with Eric Clapton were performing.

My 'Brideshead' years

Will and Hebe outside Hertford's famous Bridge of Sighs,
named after the bridge in Venice

Oxford was one of the most joyous and fulfilling periods of my
life. Among the alumni of Hertford was Evelyn Waugh, author
of *Brideshead Revisited*. And in the 1960s, the College, with
its Bridge of Sighs (modelled on its Venetian namesake) had
retained the spirit of his novel – an unambitious backwater in

149

Oxford academic life. I had made it my first choice only on the advice of my Eton housemaster, Christopher Gowan.

On the journey from Ascot to Oxford for my first term, my parents were together in the car, and not arguing for once, which was remarkable in itself. I dearly wanted the approbation of my father, but he remained quiet as we entered the college and sought out my room. I could tell he was proud, but he didn't say anything. I too tend to say nothing when I'm not sure what to say, especially if there's a chance of saying the wrong thing or causing offence. What kept my father quiet on this happy occasion I'll never know, but it was a grave disappointment to me.

Before I went up, I believed that I would struggle to raise my head above the parapet academically among a lot of very bright fellow students. I knew that the top 10% of brains got places at Oxbridge – and I did not think I belonged in that stratosphere.

There were far fewer women in those days, as three-quarters of the places were for men. My college pulled itself up by the academic bootstraps after I graduated. This was partly because Hertford was among the first colleges to accept women and also because they developed a unique interview method to find students who would get the most out of Oxford, especially in their degrees. Hertford also makes a special effort to give places to students from state schools.

Before going to Oxford, I did stupid things like selling my good collection of Elvis Presley records. I thought (or felt) they would not be respected at Oxford where, I imagined, students would be listening languorously to jazz and classical music. How wrong I was, as the first student I met on my staircase was Christopher Inge, who took me to his room to see his prized radiogram and listen to the Beach Boys (*California Dreaming*). If only I had known in advance about those *Good Vibrations*. Or, better still, I had trusted my own taste in music and not made a blind decision based on false perceptions and assumptions.

My first two years were spent in College, with a room which overlooked the Bridge of Sighs but was a longish walk to the loos and washrooms across that bridge. In my last year I moved into digs off the Iffley Road which did not have central heating – only a gas fire in the sitting room – and every morning my landlady left a jug of hot water for washing outside my room.

My idyllic student life was filled with pubs, parties, sport, card games, and reading history books. I reckon I did more work on my degree course than some of my colleagues. At Oxford, I often felt reserved, vulnerable, unconfident, and ill-at-ease in company, and I didn't like the feeling. I must have appeared aloof and arrogant. I remained the reserved introvert and felt unable to make much effort to woo women, although I did meet Susie, my future wife, before the start of my last year. And that event transformed my life.

All good things, like being a university student, must come to an end. Eventually, the week of Finals (the degree exams) arrived, and that was one of the most frightening and nerve-wracking experiences of my life. But I got through the exams and was due on a summer holiday with Susie and her family in Portugal. However, before the holiday I was summoned back to Oxford for a 'viva', an oral exam. When students' results are on the cusp between one degree grade and another they get interviewed by a panel of dons to determine which level of honours degree they are awarded. This is known as a *viva* or *viva voce*, Latin for 'with living voice'.

Having discussed my revision programme with my tutor before the viva, we agreed that I was probably on the borderline between a second and a third. "You won't get asked questions about your special subject (the Causes of the American Civil War) unless you are on the verge of a first," he told me. So I revised my special subject only superficially.

At my viva I was asked many specific questions about the start of the Civil War, and, while I remembered the answers vaguely, I had forgotten the detail – it is amazing how short the memory is for details. It turned out that the viva was for a first. That's never bothered me as I haven't got a first-class mind. I'm just good under pressure working against a deadline.

During that holiday, the results, with lists of degree levels in each subject, were published in the newspapers. I rushed to buy a copy of the *Daily Telegraph*, and found that, in the list of results for Modern History, N M Keith had got a 2nd Class Honours degree. No surprise. (Incidentally, we were staying in the same village from where Madeleine McCann was abducted many years later, so I always feel a pang whenever her name is mentioned.)

Apprenticeships

I must add as an important footnote to my Oxford experience, that university is not for everyone, even if people have the grades. I am a big fan of apprenticeships, where students can learn practical and communications skills at work while being released to attend college or university to gain academic knowledge.

There is a danger that the national obsession of going to university and getting a degree will create a society of haves and have-nots – especially in the new digital age where knowledge and AI will predominate.

Next chapter, How to find a special niche in life.

Skills and opportunities

"You gotta keep trying to find your niche and trying to fit into whatever slot that's left for you, or to make one of your own."

DOLLY PARTON

This Much I Know

- Seek and find a niche; get the career you want
- Use networking, volunteering and social media

A special niche outside home life falls into two parts: your career and your leisure time. Careers come first for most of us, and we may not have found the right one.

For all those seeking to find their niche, I turn again to Sir Ken Robinson and recommend his books, which are wise on the subjects of creative learning and finding the right job. These books include *The Element* (2009) and *Finding the Element*.

He gives excellent advice on how to find your niche, which he calls 'The Element'. He writes, "The Element is the meeting point between natural aptitude and personal passion ... (It) has two main features and there are two conditions for being in it.

The features are aptitude and passion. The conditions are attitude and opportunity. The sequence goes something like this: I get it; I love it; I want it; Where is it?"

> *"If you don't embrace the fact that you think about the world in a wide variety of ways, you severely limit your chances of finding the person that you were meant to be."*
>
> SIR KEN ROBINSON

Robinson's book has case studies of famous stars who were not academically gifted and struggled to find their niche. Sometimes it required good parents, good mentors and/or good luck. People like Mick Fleetwood of Fleetwood Mac; Paul McCartney; actress Meg Ryan; Matt Groening, creator of *The Simpsons*; choreographer Gillian Lynne; and tennis player Monica Seles.

He discusses how these famous people sought out their element, their passion; got 'in the zone' or 'in the flow' (common sports metaphors); and 'found their tribe', people like them with similar passions.

As far as intelligence is concerned, Robinson says that there are many forms and varieties of intelligence. Alfred Binet, the Frenchman who developed the IQ test for his government, intended that it would be used to detect children with special needs who required individual teaching – and not to become the standardised measurement of a narrow form of logical brainpower. Robinson proclaims that the real question is, "How are you intelligent?" – not "How intelligent are you?"

Intelligence is diverse, dynamic and distinctive, Robinson says. "If you don't embrace the fact that you think about the world in a wide variety of ways, you severely limit your chances of finding the person that you were meant to be."

His books should be on everyone's shelves, and his talks should be saved on everyone's computer or smartphone. In 2018 he has another book out called *You, Your Child and School*, which I haven't read yet, but it may be a useful addition to the Learning chapter of this book.

Get the career you want

This year has also seen the publication of a book called *Is Your School Lying to You? Get The Career You Want. Get The Life You Deserve* by Edd Williams. The author, a career consultant and 'failed comic book artist', charts how "the path to self-knowledge can be difficult.

"I wanted to be a comic book artist when I was younger but, try as I might, I simply wasn't good enough," he said in the *I* newspaper, 1 February 2018.

Williams says that he didn't get the guidance at school or university and ploughed on with his childhood ambition. "The point is that you need to understand who you are and where your abilities and interests lie."

He states that the keys to self-development and fulfilment are: understanding your aptitude (natural talent), your skills (expertise), and interests ("the feeling of wanting to know about something or someone").

"Skill is an aptitude that has been developed... Having an interest in a subject is how we can begin to define where your skills and aptitudes may take you."

The book seems to aim mainly at school and university students – "Every student is likely to be let down by their school through a combination of bad advice and stupid advice."

Nowadays, people increasingly work on a project basis, so their work contracts are for a limited time only – the length of the project. Fewer people have long-term contracts. Hardly anyone has a job for life anymore.

So, how do you *"get the career you want and the life you deserve"*?

The questions to ask in your quest for self-knowledge are:

Where do you fit in? Are you happy in your job? Where would you like to work? How important is wealth? If you could earn enough money to live on, and you had a magic wand, what career would you choose?

Everywhere I go I discover opportunities for people to re-train, even if they have reached an age when they believe that they are less employable.

Here are a few potential new ventures to consider, which may involve re-training. And I speak from the personal experience of someone whose business was sold when I was in my mid-60s, and I was not ready to retire.

Teaching English

When I re-trained to Teach English as a Foreign Language (TEFL), this took me two months of work at a local Sixth Form College. It was full on, and I did not find it easy going back to school in my 60s – lots of resistance.

Learning to teach was hard, and it increased my respect for teachers like my son Ben and his wife, Anna.

My friend Sylvia Howe, whom I met when she was Editor of *London Portrait*, persuaded me to go with her on a TEFL course at Woking College. "We might have a bit of a laugh, and it will be fun learning together," she told me.

Learning English grammar is hard work for someone who has used the language in business all his life, without thinking – for example, I never knew there were six past tenses in English (one in Japanese).

Sylvia and I were not model students. We resisted the lessons at first because we thought we knew English inside out. But I knew the language mainly from the outside. We had to learn lesson planning and, the scariest thing of all, deliver pre-planned lessons. We taught classes of non-English people who were in the UK to work, to study, or were married.

I came to realise the importance of knowing all the technicalities of the English language in order to teach it. But at the end of it, I had a diploma from Trinity College, London. That is the required qualification, along with a diploma from CELTA (Certificate in English Language Teaching to Adults), which is Cambridge-led and has surpassed TEFL as the generic term for English teachers to non-native speakers.

Both qualifications stand you in good stead. My hard-earned diploma gave me the chance to teach, and I chose to help non-native business adults with the English language, in Istanbul, and also in residential sessions at my own home during the summer vacation period, mainly to French and Italian adult students.

I wish I had discovered this career opportunity earlier. Teaching is fun and rewarding, and it gives you the chance to travel around the world, interspersing your teaching with sightseeing. This gives you enough money to cover your living costs. But, if you want to make serious money from teaching, starting and running an agency is likely to be more profitable.

I chose to teach adults, as I felt the age difference between me and school or college students would be a problem for both teacher and student. Of my students, the French students have been more committed and hard-working. The Italian clients have been charming and fun, but I have sensed that they did not necessarily want to stay the course, show commitment, practise English outside lessons, and do their homework. There has been an expectation that I would wave a magic wand and their English would be as rounded as Winston Churchill's.

Exporting

There is a much greater opportunity for British people to export their products and services than they realise. Excellent advice, help and contacts for exporting are available through the Department of International Trade (DIT), which has replaced the Department of Trade and Industry. The DIT has regular roadshows and workshops around the country, explaining the potential of exporting, and warning of some of the pitfalls.

You can research potential markets through the DIT, who also organise regular trade missions all over the world. If you decide to export, the DIT will provide you with a Trade Adviser, who will help you through the process.

As with TEFL teaching, I wish I had discovered exporting earlier. We don't realise that we, in Brand UK, are highly respected around the world for our honesty, reliability, and creativity and innovation – in areas such as design, construction, engineering, project management, IT, services, and social media (among others).

Our perception of battered brand UK has not been borne out by my experiences in Turkey, teaching English to non-native speakers.

The learning industry is a billion-dollar global business. The first accredited school teaching English opened a century ago. And, in 2014, the revenue of the UK's English Language Teaching (ELT) sector was £1.2 billion (US$1.74 billion), according to a study.

The total economic impact of the sector – including student spending on tuition, accommodation, and other living expenses, as well as the knock-on effects of spending by ELT centres and their employees and suppliers – was estimated at £2.4 billion (US$3.48 billion). The sector supports roughly 26,650 jobs throughout the UK and returns a net tax contribution of £194 million (US$281 million) to government coffers. In 2014, there were more English language teaching jobs in the UK than at Coca-Cola or Vodafone.

The demand is out there and, whatever the outcome of the Brexit negotiations, it will remain. English, after all, is the language of business. It will continue to be used in Europe, China and the Far East. Incidentally, I have found that European business people who go and work in China often have to improve English before they can have the lessons in Mandarin or another Chinese language.

Why Istanbul? I chose to teach in Istanbul after going on a trade visit in 2014, my first trip there for many years. The city has a magnificent heritage and a natural and open import/export culture. It felt the right place for me as a newly qualified teacher, working outside the hotspots of Europe where there were scores of trained English teachers in every city and town (teachers who were more experienced, younger and better looking than me!).

In Istanbul, I joined the British Chamber of Commerce in Turkey (BCCT) who provided me with contacts and introductions, and office space in their HQ overlooking the Bosphorus. BCCT works closely with DIT staff in the British Consulate in Istanbul, where I used to host English workshops. You have no idea of the connectedness of the members of the British foreign service and their staff. However, I would add that there is no substitute for visiting and even living in your target export country, even having an office there.

To succeed at exporting takes time, patience and regular personal contact with your prospects and clients. Businesses abroad need to establish and maintain personal trust and to prove that their products and services are efficient, reliable, innovative and problem solving.

Finding opportunities

There are many other niche opportunities, but how do you find them? I call this process 'Finding NEMO' and, in this instance, NEMO stands for New Employment or Managerial Opportunities. I recommend that you:

- Go networking
- Volunteer
- Attend events, seminars and workshops
- Use social media

Networking

There are a huge number and range of networking groups. Check online, and a good place to start is at your local Chamber of

Commerce. These vary in value from town to town and area to area. But they will have a network of businesses on their database and should hold monthly networking meetings, where you can meet your fellow business folk (usually SMEs) and share your challenges and successes.

Again it takes time to build trust and relationships. You can usually try for free some of the well-known networking groups, like BNI.

There are also plenty of networking groups for women. For me, women have got the skill and value of networking much better than many men. My current favourite, Fabulous Women Marvellous Men (FWMM), was founded for women only but now encourages men to become members. Groups hold monthly meetings, mainly in London and the South East, and the network is spreading. Within a year I have started to get work through this network, whose meetings are warm, open, and fun.

Volunteering: Careers advice in schools

In recent years I have found volunteering a very useful way to meet new contacts. You also give back to society and the community, and in return, you make new friends, acquaintances and contacts.

As I said above, my current voluntary body of choice is educational, aiming to provide students with a clear pathway into jobs through school, college and university – through meetings with business people, exhibitions, seminars, and 'joined up' careers guidance. This initiative is run through the Careers & Enterprise Company (CEC).

Bearing in mind that business often complains about the skills gap found in new recruits from school, college and university, I have found this provides a great chance to help students find the best career opportunities, boost my brand, and expand my network.

I volunteer as an Enterprise Adviser (EA) with the CEC, which has set up a national network, connecting 1,700 schools and colleges with 2,000 businesses, to create career opportunities for students. The aim of CEC is to focus career guidance and help young people prepare for the world of work.

This new initiative to 'join up' careers advice in schools is the outcome of a report by Sir John Holman to the Gatsby Foundation. Sir John and his team visited five independent schools with a good reputation for career guidance (Berkhamsted School; Downe House; King Edward VI, Birmingham; Dulwich College, London; and Magdalen College School, Oxford). They also looked at the career guidance system in six countries or states – Finland, Ireland, Hong Kong, the Netherlands, and Ontario, Canada.

As a result, the report has recommended eight Gatsby Benchmarks for secondary schools (and Sixth Form Colleges). From September 2018 schools are tasked by the government to follow these benchmarks as part of their career strategy. And schools will be judged on their careers guidance performance in future OFSTED reports.

The Gatsby Benchmarks include:

- Having a stable careers programme in schools
- Learning from the labour market
- Addressing the needs of each pupil
- Linking the curriculum to careers
- Facilitating meetings between students and business people (potential employers)

- Work experience
- Encounters with further education
- Personal guidance and mentoring

For me, this marks a great, and logical step forward, and goes some way to meeting the educational vision of Sir Ken Robinson.

Moreover, the CEC has been set up to support the efforts of schools by providing help from, and contacts with, the world of business. Volunteer EAs are often senior business people, and many are CEOs and company directors. The role of the EA is to:

- Work with a school's senior leadership and careers teams to develop a strategy that gives students opportunities to get to know the world of work.
- Use their network to open doors and create more work encounters.

They get training, personal development, and peer support from other volunteers, and networking events.

With the support of an expert coordinator from LEP Solent, I advise Wildern School, Hedge End, near Southampton, which has 2,000 students and a good record in careers guidance. In volunteering for about three hours a month, I have meetings with the careers team, and we discuss the careers strategy and programme. I also attend events at Wildern during the school year such as: a Careers Fair in October; a speed networking event in January; *Dragons Den* in the Spring; and Mock interviews in June.

Being an EA has been a challenging, exciting and rewarding task for me for two years. It has proved a great opportunity to give back to students and the educational sector while expanding my network and improving my own learning and skills.

In 2018 I have started as a mentor to students at a local Sixth Form College. They will take their A levels in 2019 and are preparing for interviews at the universities of their choice. I and a number of other graduates have the job of improving their confidence to talk about a wide number of subjects. Since the college introduced this mentoring process in recent years, they have found that their students have much more success in getting places at Oxbridge and other leading universities in the UK.

Events and seminars

I am bombarded with opportunities through my online networks and emails, and through the networking events I attend. Chambers of Commerce and your LEP are good sources of information on business fairs, and they stage events themselves. Eventbrite is an online event organising outfit.

Social media

As a place to seek opportunities, social media is more of a challenge. And, if you get into social media, you have to be extremely productive and positive. For me, Facebook remains more of a social network, although business groups often have a presence on FB where you can see and discuss issues.

Twitter is interesting but has not quite cut the mustard yet. LinkedIn seems a bit stodgy to me, a place to recruit staff and also keep in touch with people's progress; and some people have found it a valuable area for finding a job or an employee. WhatsApp groups are proliferating, and some of them are high-powered and information-filled. Avid social networkers also recommend Instagram, but I have not yet engaged with that.

Of course, there are perils in sticking your head above the parapet online. We have all heard of the scams and the trolls.

For me, it is a question of staying informed of those dangers and trying to steer clear of them. Some of the scams are so realistic that I have been tempted by them. Remember to think twice about any offer which looks too good to be true (it probably is); or the person or organisation who you don't know, and which has no address, and asks for money upfront. Caveat emptor or your coffers will be empty.

The next chapter meets the challenges of health and fitness.

Fitness, food, illness and exercise

*"It is health that is real wealth
not pieces of gold and silver."*

MAHATMA GANDHI

What I've Learnt

- Take your health and fitness seriously
- Take regular exercise
- Take regular blood tests and annual medical check-ups

Emotions are inextricably linked to health. When asked the question, 'How are you?' we tend to reply: 'I feel fine, thank you?' Or 'I don't feel so good at the moment.' We also say: 'I feel sick' and 'My throat feels sore.' While these physical symptoms may not be strictly emotional, we have made the connection in the language. It seems certain that our emotions affect our health. Prevailing moods of fear, anger, anxiety and other negative emotions lead to illnesses, which can be fatal.

Besides, we connect health (and wealth) with happiness. For most people, including me, health is a significantly more important factor in my happiness than wealth. For, without good health, we can't enjoy life or any wealth we have. It's so hard to be happy without good health.

Physical health

If you are physically fit and healthy, you are likely to have a wealth of spiritual contentment. That is a given. However, nowadays there is so much health information and so many tips, online and in print, that it is extremely hard to make sense of it all.

Much of the good and the bad is connected to food: what we eat, how we eat, when eat, how much we eat, where we eat. In 2017, top of the nutritional pops were aspirin, coffee, and five-a-day diets. Bottom of the polls were sugar and dietary drinks. Alcohol, in moderation, has had mixed reports, with fluctuating scientific evidence as to whether it is really bad for you or moderately good for you.

Frankly, I'm a fan of the TV doctor Michael Mosley, whose BBC series *Trust Me I'm a Doctor*, and other documentaries frequently uncover misconceptions or misinterpretations of the scientific evidence – about health, eating and exercise. Science research is constantly finding new things about familiar topics. So the answer is to use your common sense and don't immediately adopt each new health and medical miracle.

Indeed I take it all with a pinch of salt. Oh, no, I can't do that, because too much salt is bad for you!

Illness, diseases and accidents

The most onerous health issues are prolonged and life-limiting illnesses and serious accidents. I don't know about you, but I find it very hard to express my feelings in a helpful way to someone who is seriously ill.

Fortunately, I have not had to face such a problem personally. But I admire people who get up and do battle with illness or injury. The mind is a powerful tool, and I like to think that I would be a fighter if I contracted a major illness.

Easier said than done, of course, and the option to combat an illness or accident may not be available. Stories are uplifting of the many people who recover enough from a debilitating condition to lead a reasonably normal life or even take part in Paralympic sport.

We had a great friend, Mrs T (Veronica Thomas), who was diagnosed with motor neurone disease while she was a school matron. While she had to leave her job, she lived many more years than was predicted, and enjoyed a full life, because her strong spirit kept her going until the end. Not everyone has the will or the way to be a Mrs T.

Topic of Cancer

Both my parents died of liver cancer. My older half-brother, Bobby Barbour, was struck down by prostate cancer and died just before his 65th birthday. Originally, he noticed pains in his back and thought he had pulled some back muscles playing ping pong.

Men of his generation, and mine, do not tend to go and see a doctor if they experience a physical problem and pain. The Macmillan nurses who looked after him were remarkable. I asked one of them whether she ever felt sad watching her patients drift down towards death. She said, no, because there was always a transcendent moment of grace when the dying person accepted their situation, gave up their war against illness, and accepted their peaceful fate. Bobby had been fighting, fighting. But that moment of graceful peace and acceptance finally arrived. That was more than 25 years ago.

Only this year Bill Turnbull, the popular former BBC Breakfast TV presenter, announced that he had been diagnosed with advanced prostate cancer. He admitted he had been slow in going to see his GP with the aches and pains he was suffering – which he put down to getting old.

My first ever experience of hospital as an adult was when I had a urinary problem 20 years ago, and I had an operation on a benign prostate. It had grown so large that it was pressing on my bladder, and I was getting up several times in the night to urinate.

Eventually I became incontinent and had to wear a nappy at night. Since then I have had annual blood tests for prostate cancer because you are a candidate if a relative has suffered from the disease.

In the news

Prostate cancer has hit the headlines in 2018 with the revelation that "The number of men dying from prostate cancer has overtaken female deaths from breast cancer for the first time in the UK." (BBC News: http://www.bbc.co.uk/news/health-42890405)

"An ageing population means more men are developing and dying from the disease. Prostate Cancer UK says advances in the diagnosis and treatment of breast cancer are paying off, and increased funding could benefit prostate cancer. The biggest cancer killers in the UK remain lung and bowel cancer.

"The latest figures from 2015 show there were 11,819 deaths from prostate cancer compared with 11,442 from breast cancer.

Although deaths from prostate cancer have been rising over the past 10 years or so, the mortality rate, the proportion of men dying from the disease, has fallen by 6% between 2010 and 2015. For breast cancer the mortality rate has come down by 10%, meaning deaths in women are declining more quickly."

The Daily Mail caused a media storm when it reported that prostate cancer "receives far less research spending than breast cancer." And it stated in big bold type at the start of an article by Amanda Platell...

"Men STILL dying of embarrassment: Fears over 'masculinity' and discussing intimate problems stop prostate patients visiting the doctor"

http://www.dailymail.co.uk/news/article-5351597/Prostate-cancer-victims-dying-embarrassment.html/

The answer is: if in pain or in doubt, seek medical advice. And don't take no for an answer. Get a second opinion if you don't find useful or convincing medical advice.

Arthritis: Hippy, hippy shakes

Problems with my hips have proved my biggest medical problem in the last 10 years. I have had five hip replacements: four on the left hip and one on the right. The first four were on my left hip. First, I underwent a Birmingham hip replacement in 2009, paid for by medical insurance in a private hospital near Southampton. After a year, that hip was causing huge pain, and the Birmingham had not worked, so I had a replacement for the replacement by the same surgeon, Jeremy Latham. This operation was on the NHS in Southampton General Hospital.

Only weeks after that op, in July 2010, I was recuperating nicely at home when I fell over in the garden on a warm summer's evening and broke the left hip in several places. I was taken by ambulance to the nearest NHS hospital, St Richard's in Chichester, and there I had another replacement, metal on metal (and that was to prove significant six years later).

A length of metal was inserted into my hip to hold the bone together where it entered the hip socket. All went well until early 2016 when I was working in Istanbul, where I was teaching English, and without warning collapsed in the street in great pain one Saturday.

I thought I had dislocated the hip, or the implant had somehow failed. However, a scan in the American hospital in Istanbul on the Monday revealed no obvious damage to the implant or the hip.

Advised to return to the UK for a complete check, the senior consultant at St Richard's took one look at my situation and wrote 'metal poisoning' in my notes. A blood test showed that it was metal poisoning (metallosis). I had 30 times as much metal in my body as normal.

The two metal units had rubbed together and released tiny fragments of metal into my bloodstream and soft tissue. Eventually, these had formed a metallic 'cowpat' on the hip (under the skin), and this had caused my fall. The metal was removed, and the hip replaced for a fourth time with metal on ceramic/plastic.

I was told by the fracture team at St Richard's that they could not remove all the metal, and that it was up to my natural body functions to clear my system. So the metal might never be flushed out. Disconcertingly they said that they did not know whether I would have any after-effects. I can only say that my muscles have been weakened ever since, and whatever exercise I take I have been unable to restore my body back to its old self.

So how do I feel about all this? Physically, I have far less energy, and I have to walk slowly; after one hour, I feel exhausted. My muscles ache on a daily basis, and I feel generally debilitated. Gone, for now at least, is the prospect of resuming one of my favourite hobbies, fell walking in the hills of the Lake District. Emotionally I feel frustrated and cross that the medical experts can't do more to help me out of this condition. Yet my spirits remain high, so I am stoically 'counting my blessings'. A very British state of mind!

Health hazard

As a footnote I would add a word of warning to any readers, or their acquaintances, facing hip surgery. Metal on metal hips are potentially dangerous to patients as some 5% of people develop metallosis.

These types of hip replacements have been around for some time, but about 15 years ago the manufacturers made an extra effort in their sales pitch to hospitals. Apparently, it was said that metal on metal hips would last longer than the 15 or so years for which other traditional methods endured.

What the manufacturers failed to reveal was some internal research which had indicated that some after-effects might develop over time for some patients. This has all come to light in a British Medical Journal (BMJ) report which accused manufacturers of hiding the evidence of the dangers of metal on metal hips. The report examined "the evidence of risk from metal-on-metal hips, the manufacturers' inadequate response, and how the regulatory bodies failed to give doctors and patients the information they need to make informed decisions." https://www.bmj.com/content/344/bmj.e1410/

Some 60,000 people in the UK are suffering from post-operative hip problems. Many hundreds of thousands of people are involved in class actions in the UK and the US. Generally, of course, hip replacements give added life to older people's ageing limbs.

As I get older, however, I find that my balance gets worse and my clumsiness increases. This is just another symptom of age, and I try to walk more carefully to avoid the occasional falls, which result in my head-butting the pavement and/or cutting my hands and knees.

Fit to burst

Keeping fit is one of the big challenges of modern times when we are all inclined to lead more sedentary lives than in past generations. Then people were more disposed to walk or cycle to work or to the shops. And if we used public transport (because fewer of us owned cars), we had to walk to the bus or train station.

Before the arrival of mechanical transport, walking or riding a horse were the only transport options. The Victorian Prime Minister William Gladstone, one of my historical heroes, used to take the train from London to a station near his home in Hawarden Castle, on the Welsh border with Cheshire. Then he thought nothing of walking the 15 miles from the station to his house. And he often spent the weekends chopping up wood.

These kinds of lifestyles were typical, and they meant that, even if someone could afford to eat heartily, their natural exercise patterns kept them fit – until they were struck down at an early age by poverty or a disease for which science had not found a cure. Today we espouse the disciplines of walking, swimming, cycling, running, horse riding, sport, and/or the gym.

Dr Mosley delighted me in a recent BBC programme when he found that strenuous exercise for short periods was just as effective in keeping people fit as hours running on the road or in the park, and training in the gym. It is also said that walking briskly for 30 minutes (so that you are hot and slightly out of breath) is good for your fitness.

Diet and food

Obesity is one of the big bugbears of our age, and the problem is getting worse, especially among young people. While I have always struggled with my weight, and I could lose a few pounds, I don't consider myself to be obese.

A study of 225,000 obese people for 16 years by Harvard and Boston Universities confirmed that they were more likely to die before their time, specifically from heart problems. This overturned other research, which had found that obesity would not cause such people to die earlier than fitter folk.

Diet is just as important as exercise. "You can't have one without the other," as the song goes. Ah, but that's in Frank Sinatra's *Love and Marriage* from a previous chapter.

Anyway, a ration of five-a-day from a selection of fruit and vegetables is recommended by the experts, although some fruits are better for your weight and your waistline than others – mainly berries and citrus fruit. Research suggests that only 25% of UK adults achieve this five-a-day target.

However, now you may have to double up to ten-a-day. Research by Imperial College London of 2 million people has found that eating 200 grams of fruit and veg (2.5 portions) a day reduced the risk of early death by 15%; while 800g cuts the risk by 31%.

For people (like me) who love all sorts of food and are happy to eat their five-a-day, it is a relief to know that a balanced diet ought to keep us healthy – because it's wise. Moderation in all things may not be so easy to achieve.

My early childhood was spent without much chocolate, because of rationing after the War, and I was not much of a fan of chocolate or sweets – apart from liquorice and sherbet. As I have grown older, I have bouts of bingeing on chocolate. The answer is to resist buying chocolate or biscuits, so they are not in the house to tempt.

Mark Twain had a wry remark about staying healthy: "The only way to keep your health is to eat what you don't want, drink what you don't like, and do what you'd rather not."

A recent book by Ruby Tandoh, a British baker, made famous by BBC's *Bake Off,* has given us greater licence to enjoy a wider range of foods, without getting stuck in faddy diets, which are usually unsuccessful in the long term. Her 2018 book *Eat UP* maintains that "Eating is one of life's greatest pleasures. Food nourishes our bodies, helps us celebrate our successes (from a wedding cake to a post-night out kebab), cheers us up when we're down, introduces us to new cultures and - when we cook and eat together - connects us with the people we love."

How many people do you know who go on a strict diet of one sort or another, lose a lot of weight, and then put it all back on again? My parents recalled their experiences at health farms in the 1950s – famous commuter belt establishments like Forest Mere and Enton Hall – where they watched couples fastidiously nibbling a piece of celery and sipping water all day. They even skipped mealtimes but dashed out to their Jaguar cars to slurp tumblers of gin and tonic, and wolf down bread, cheese and chocolate, washed down with great goblets of wine.

Without doubt, the most enjoyable healthy diets are Mediterranean or Eastern, with plenty of olive oil, fresh vegetables, and nuts, seeds and spices. I can certainly live with that.

Alzheimer's

People talk about the universe 'looking after you' or 'looking out for you'. They say, 'Ask the universe for help, and see what happens'. I have to say that I've been slightly sceptical, although, in the past, I have never completely dismissed the notion.

However I think the universe seems to have been on my side, unbidden, throughout the process of writing this book. Whenever I have struggled to find the words to talk about a topic, there has been an item of news, a radio or television programme, or a new book has appeared to provide a lead.

Take the question of Alzheimer's, which is just one of the many forms of dementia. Although I have had little first-hand experience of dementia or Alzheimer's, I did witness it in my mother and Geraldine's mother. They are among the illnesses of old age which are the most dreaded.

In the week when I sat down to write about these problems, *Book of the Week* on BBC Radio 4 broadcast five 15-minute excerpts from a new book by Wendy Mitchell. The author was diagnosed with early onset Alzheimer's at the age of 58. She had to give up her job, remove mirrors in her house because the strange face concerned her, and write Post-it Notes each day to remind her what she had to do and what she was planning to be doing it.

Then she decided to write a blog, which has become her new book – *Somebody I used to know*, co-written with Anna Wharton. Reviewer Rosie Boycott said, "An extraordinary book about a little-understood disease." *The Financial Times* testimonial reads, "Awe-inspiring, courageous and insightful. I would recommend it to everyone."

"It's like I'm not there"

Here's a short excerpt from Wendy's book transcribed from a reading by Tessa Gallagher.

"People often ask me what it's like to have dementia on a bad day. But it's hard to remember. It's like I'm not there. On those days I can feel the disease in my head like it's eating away at all that's good in there.

"There's no clarity from the moment I open my eyes. Where am I? My own handwriting on the notepad beside my bed is a mystery. On those days there is little in my brain to help me through.

"It's as if it has been emptied overnight and restored to factory settings. The key is always calm thoughts. Waiting and looking at anything that distracts me from the fog: photographs, a hill, a lake, a daughter.

"It's not just what I can't see. It's what I can see too, what I think is real but it's just an illusion. One morning I came downstairs and looked out at my back garden. My shed had gone. There was a blank where it once was, just a concrete base. I could have panicked then and called the police to register the crime. Instead, I told myself I would go back in 30 minutes. If it still wasn't there, I would know it was real. Later the shed was there. Of course, it was. But this kind of thing happens a lot."

To learn more first-hand about Alzheimer's and dementia, Wendy's brave book makes excellent reading.

Alcohol and drugs

Earlier in the chapter, I joked about the scientific findings on alcohol. But I know from personal experience that alcoholism is a big problem, both for alcoholics and for the families and friends. Both my parents were alcoholics.

In those days, drinking and smoking heavily were part of the normal social scene. In 2018 there has been a new campaign, launched by Labour MP Liam Byrne, to focus on the plight of children of alcoholic parents. Chairman of the All-Party Group on the Children of Alcoholics.

He wrote in *The Guardian* in February 2018 that, two years ago, he held the hand of his alcoholic father "as he slipped away. In the weeks that followed, I knew I had to start speaking out about the plight of children of alcoholics. All two million of them." **http://bit.ly/2nVFJ1w**

I have to say this state of affairs was part of my life growing up. Whether it affected me greatly, I don't know. I'm not blaming it for anything in particular, although the irrational arguments and noise of drunken parents may have had some effect. For me, alcohol is a drug which is just as dangerous, if not more so, than banned substances, because it is legal and socially acceptable.

Re-ablement

I have just embarked on a series of 're-ablement' exercise classes, devised by the physio team in a local hospital. Once a week on Mondays I attend the two-hour exercise classes in the hospital to stretch, bend, march, lift, balance – sitting and standing –

working on toes, heels, ankles, legs, knees, hips, back, arms, shoulders, neck, and central core muscles. A sheet is provided to undertake 40 minutes of this workout at home three times a week.

Next chapter, Travel liberates you and adventure inspires.

CHAPTER TEN

ADVENTURES

How travel liberates you

"I believe that adventure is about stretching yourself,
mentally, physically and culturally...
Adventure is only a state of mind."

ALISTAIR HUMPHREYS, GLOBAL ADVENTURER

This Much I Know

- Travel liberates, and adventure inspires
- Meeting new people is uplifting and makes you feel better
- Local 'micro' adventures are equally rewarding

As I wrote in the Introduction, travel and my adventures in India and Australia last winter have inspired this book. There is no doubt that travelling can make you feel much better, about yourself and about the world, spiritually and mentally.

In the past, I always thought that travel was just a lovely luxury. 'It broadens the mind', the old cliché goes. Now I appreciate from my own experiences that travel means much more than that – and adventure has a much greater impact on the spirit. It does not have to be a big adventure. Small, local adventures can be great fun and just as rewarding.

If you have time to spend significant time travelling, at home or abroad, that could make a huge difference to how you feel. But that is only going to happen once in a blue moon – in your gap year before or after university when you are young, or on a sabbatical when you have worked for one company for some time, or in retirement.

When you are young, your eyes may not be open to all the subtle gifts that travel can bring, because you simply don't have the experience. When you are older, there is more chance. However, it is likely that only once in a lifetime will you spend a long period – one, two or three months, say, on sabbatical – plunged deeply and wholehearted into an adventurous travel experience.

When I worked at *The Times*, I had a sabbatical, but I spent my time writing a sports book. Indeed many journalists I know have spent time off writing books. Chance wasted.

My eyes were fully opened in 2017 when I took that special trip to India and then Australia. The first 12 days of my Indian adventure were with a group. The camaraderie and the close community added to the experience. This was an adventure, not a holiday, a trip or a journey.

Often on a long holiday, you travel with family, friends, or on your own. And I found the experience of travelling in India from Delhi to Goa in a group sharpened the experience, with the novelty of having fresh faces and unfamiliar voices around you.

I travelled with G Adventures, and I booked the tour with that company, and the flights separately, early in 2017. I arrived in Delhi on 11th October, three days before the group was scheduled to meet up and did some sightseeing on my own.

> When choosing your travel company, it is
> important to be in the company of a good-sized
> group. A great friend of mine went on a tour of
> India where she was one of only three people in the
> group. The other two were a married couple who
> fought like Bengal tigers throughout.

From the start, I felt relaxed and ready to meet challenges and disappointments. My first challenge came as soon as I opened my suitcase in the hotel in Delhi. It was not my suitcase; accidentally I had collected the wrong one from the baggage carousel. The case belonged to a woman.

Shrugging off the disappointment of having no clean clothes to wear, I went to bed, got up in my travel-worn clothes the next morning, and took the hotel taxi to Delhi Airport. I felt peaceful and patient.

There was some farcical bureaucracy: the airport authorities had my passport but insisted on photographing my passport photo and creating a childlike ID card. But I was finally reunited with my case in a subterranean customs office only after two hours when I was moved from one office to another and back, had photocopies and documents, signed copious papers, and had conversations with customs officials in several different areas.

Indian ink

I recorded my adventures in India in a WhatsApp blog which I cunningly called Indian Ink. The five highlights of my Indian adventure were:

1) The Taj Mahal
2) Diwali in Udaipur
3) The slums in Mumbai
4) Green and gorgeous Kerala
5) India's airports

The G Adventures group at the Taj Mahal

I was fully expecting the Taj Mahal to disappoint as I had heard so much about it. But it proved to be a truly wonderful and a spiritually uplifting experience.

The group was up at 5am and in the queue 30 minutes before the Taj Mahal opened at 6am. The gates duly opened at dawn, and we all rushed to the entrance. There we were greeted by one of the magical wonders of the world. The peace and grandeur took my breath away and, having walked around it and through it, I sat down on a bench to contemplate life, mine and the lives of others.

Fine sights and fireworks

The next highlight was Diwali, the festival of light, when we were in Udaipur, the city of love and the lake. There we enjoyed tours of the City Palace, the lake at sunset and a studio for miniature paintings.

At a studio, we had miniatures painted on our thumbnails. Mine was a tiger (representing courage). Other people had an elephant (good luck), a horse (power), a camel (love), a peacock (beauty), or a cow (holiness).

However, the undoubted highlight of our stay was the Diwali celebrations with bright illuminations and a non-stop private firework display, on and off for 24 hours. The festival means different things to different people and is associated with a number of Hindu gods and goddesses.

"Diwali is a Hindu festival with lights, held in the period from October to November. It is particularly associated with Lakshmi, the goddess of prosperity, and marks the beginning of the financial year in India."

Below is an invocation of Diwali from an Indian acquaintance.

A meaning of Diwali

It is Diwali, and I thank you for walking the earth in part of my journey and pray you make it a better place.

As we light our houses today, spend some time lighting a few lamps inside you and sit in silence with our eyes closed... Om x

Light the 1st lamp inside your mind and let it burn any anger/jealousy that you may have for anyone... See it melt away...

Light the 2nd lamp in your gut and let it burn away unwanted greed and desires...

Feel happy and content with what you have been blessed with.

Light the 3rd lamp and let it fade away all insecurities or fears that you may have built up in your mind about health, financials or people.

Just believe in the power which gave you life will surely give you enough to survive.

Light the 4th lamp and carry that lamp to each part of your precious body; let it burn away all diseased cells.

Feel yourself as healthy as this lamp travels to each body part and illuminates each organ.

Picture the 5th lamp as a mini Sun... nothing but divine light... Light it in the centre of your body and let it fill its warmth and love inside your whole body...

Feel at one with the Divine... Let the love and warmth filled inside you ooze out of you through your smile... eyes... speech... and body... carry this love with you always...

The biggest blessing is that whoever meets you becomes happier through your infectious being... and this will make you even happier in return

Light these 5 lamps each morning and carry their positivity wherever you go...

Wish you and your dearest a very enlightening Happy Diwali... and a most Magical Hindu New Year.

I Love You and You must too... it's the best feeling in the world.

Kalpesh Patel
www.iJustDoit.com

Note: This is just one version of Diwali among thousands, but I love the simple spirituality. Indeed the whole Hindu pantheon of holy spirits is one big atmospheric nirvana – an idyllic place.

Mumbai slums

My third treasured experience in India was an escorted tour of the Mumbai slum called Dharavi, meaning 'flowing river'. This was very similar to (if not the set of) Danny Boyle's film *Slumdog Millionaire*. A small party of five westerners was shown round by Juti Jain, who was brought up in Dharavi. When his father was two, he and his family had been re-homed there after a natural disaster had wrecked their village.

The inhabitants are proud and independent people. There are three schools and a public hospital, which gives what is described as 'lower quality care'. No begging happens, and tourists are not allowed to take photographs.

The area is the equivalent size of 500 soccer pitches or half of Central Park, New York. There are only four toilets for the whole population, who, if they are lucky, live in accommodation which measures 10 square metres. The many small industries include plastic recycling (the whole process starts in the slums), aluminium melting, soap recycling, mechanical processes, garment making, and scores of foundries.

The work is done by people who come to Mumbai from the countryside (and go back home at harvest time). They earn about £100 a week to send home, and they live in their small Dickensian factory spaces, which also serve as dormitories and often have no natural light. The male inhabitants of Dharavi go out into Mumbai to work, plying whatever trade they may have.

The main role of women is to stay at home and look after their small homes and their children. They can use their hand skills to make bags, garments, and bread and pastry. Some have started to become teachers. We were proudly shown one of the three schools in the slum.

Our guide Juti told us that the authorities have to get 70% approval from inhabitants if they want to destroy a section of slums for redevelopment. Often the local people vote against it. His father was extremely concerned when he had the chance to move out to new premises. He dreaded losing his friendly community and his work as a tailor. However, he did agree, and things have turned out well for him because he has set up a tailoring business.

From these extraordinary sights in Mumbai, I flew to Kochi. There I met my driver, and we set off on a tranquil week in Kerala, one of the more developed states in India, where 92% of children go to primary school, and the literacy rate is very high. Kerala has benefited from high human development compared with low economic development. With rice production declining, the Kerala economy runs at a large deficit and relies upon grants from central government. The main products are coir, rubber, cashew nuts, spices, and a burgeoning service industry includes the first Information Technology Park in India.

Environmentally rich and exotic, Kerala has a lush green landscape with an abundance of wild flowers, and tea plantations on the rolling hills (established by two Englishmen in the 19th century). Indeed it was the English who introduced tea to India, along with democracy, the civil service, railways and cricket. In that sense colonialism had some benefits, although the colonists' treatment of local people, places and possessions was not so admirable – as much pillaging and raping, as peaceful development.

Flights of fancy

Finally, a word of praise for the airports in the sub-continent. In the knowledge that transport will help to transform the economy and facilitate the international digital status it aspires to, India has invested thoroughly and thoughtfully. The airports are magnificent cathedrals for creativity, and I happily spent a whole day in Bengaluru airport, working, reading, eating and watching TV in its wide open spaces.

Imagine doing all that with pleasure in a British airport, which tend to have too many people and too few facilities, unless you can get into a business lounge. The scope of India's airports for the average passenger makes many of those in Europe look decidedly third world.

Australia fair

After India, the adventure continued in Australia, throughout November 2017. First, I enjoyed the Melbourne Cup, a nation-stopping horse race which happens on the second Tuesday in November. It is celebrated as a public holiday in Victoria, and the whole of Australia stops to enjoy the spectacle.

Australians insist the day is like the English FA Cup Final, the Grand National, and the Derby all rolled into one. But in the UK, we don't have a public holiday for any of those big sporting events.

The Melbourne Cup was an excellent day, with everyone in the 100,000 crowd apparently having fun, and not much sign of racegoers becoming 'tired and emotional' with alcohol. The race result was an Irish family affair with the winner, Rekindling, trained by Joseph O'Brien and the second horse, Johannes Vermeer, trained by his father, Aidan.

Foolishly, I backed the favourite, an Australian-trained horse, Almandin, ridden by Frankie Dettori. But I had some joy with a fifth-place each-way bet on Nakeeta. What I've learnt is that you should back horses with experience of running in Australia, and preferably ridden by a local jockey, as were the O'Brien duo.

As well as the racing I also enjoyed the Melbourne tram system. Founded on money from the Gold Rush in the 1850s, the city seems dignified and slightly old-fashioned. A Melbourne-born Australian friend who now lives in Sydney told me that the best way to annoy residents of his native city is to praise the home of the Opera House. And the best way to irritate Sydney folk is to compliment Melbourne.

My adventure moved on to Sydney where I was a sight-seer in the city's breathtaking harbour and enjoyed a live performance at

Sydney Opera House. Ferry trips and car journeys to see a few of the city's hundreds of beaches completed the picture.

The third and final stay was in Brisbane, scene of the first Ashes Test between Australia and England. I attended on four of the five days, although by the end of the match it was clear that England had been soundly beaten after a good start. I enjoyed staying with new friends, Franck and Sophie Begon, in their little French quarter in a Brisbane suburb. Franck is a French engineer who works for Airbus, while Sophie's mother is French.

The couple have bought a plot of land with a house, imported another property, rebuilt it and let it as an Airbnb. They have dubbed their property Versailles, and the three of us spent many a happy hour imagining how they would declare independence for their Versailles, and called the new state Begonia. So that made an easy choice for a national flower and an outline design for a flag. When I left them they were busy writing a constitution. They told me that one problem was that land in Brisbane is technically Crown property, so they would have to swear allegiance to our Queen.

'Advance Australia fair' is how the national anthem goes. The climate, sunshine and weather are certainly as fair as fair can be. My mental, physical and cultural stretch had certainly made India and Australia genuine adventures.

'Even the bad times are good'

In this adventure, even the bad times were good or at least turned out well. After the wrong luggage incident in Delhi at the start, I had a second misadventure which happened at the end of the long flight home to the UK. I unwittingly dropped my phone on the way to the loo. Back in my seat I searched for the phone, found it was missing, and scrabbled on the floor looking under other seats as best I could. When the plane landed, I did not disembark immediately but stayed behind to continue my search for the phone with the cabin crew. No success.

In Heathrow Airport arrivals I reported that my phone had gone missing to the airline desk but guessed that someone had picked it up and pocketed it, so that was the last I would see of it. Next morning I woke and prepared to go through the process of ordering another phone. Lo and behold there was a message in my email inbox telling me that I was due for an update. So I quickly went to the server's shop in my local high street, cancelled the old phone, and bought a new one. Easy.

Locations I love

Other favourite places for adventure include Ireland, Yorkshire, The Lake District, and Istanbul. The first three places are domestic idylls for me. I have also spent some time recently teaching English to business people in Istanbul, which is my favourite city in the world.

In all these places I can stretch myself mentally, and physically. The benefits are meeting other people, embracing new cultures, getting insights into different ways of working and living, sensing new smells and sounds, seeing colours and sights differently, and learning about different philosophies and religions.

What about safety? When I was a teacher in Istanbul for two years from 2014-16, friends were forever asking me whether I felt worried or scared living and working in a foreign city where there were terrorist shootings and bombings. I simply replied that: a) Istanbul was probably no more dangerous than London or Paris, where many terrorists lived; and b) I kept my eyes and ears open, staying away from terrorist targets such as groups of tourists, the police, and the American embassy

The two memorable incidents in Turkey, while I was living there, were the bombing of a group of tourists near the Blue Mosque, and a gun attack on New Year's Eve at a nightclub overlooking the Bosphorous at the suburb of Ortakoy near where I lived. The nightclub attack did give me cause to think, as outside was a bus stop where I used to disembark after coming back from the centre of Istanbul. But, if it was late at night, I took a taxi. Staying safe is common sense, and I believe that fortune plays a part in whether you are in the right or the wrong place at any given moment in your life. Besides, I quickly learned to love Istanbul. It has become one of my favourite cities.

I moved back home because the political and economic uncertainties under the authoritarian President Recep Erdogan have meant that work opportunities have dried up for non-native business trainers and teachers like me. Whenever I can, I return to Istanbul and revisit my old haunts and catch up with good friends, usually in Leo's U2 Irish pub near Taksim Square where they sell the best Guinness outside Dublin.

As I have written, I find the mosques of Istanbul the most spiritual of places, because they are simple and holy with none of the distractions of wealth and ornateness of many churches and temples.

Inside Islam

The second largest religion in the world, Islam has 1 billion followers, Muslims. The Arabic word Islam means submission to the will of Allah (God). Muhammad, the messenger of Allah, received the word more than 1400 years ago in Mecca.

He was the last prophet of God, following in the footsteps of Jesus, Moses and Abraham.

The holy book of Islam is the Qur'an, dictated to Muhammad by Allah. Its Five Pillars of faith are:

The declaration of faith

Praying five times a day

Giving money to charity

Fasting

At least one pilgrimage to Mecca

Inside a mosque is a world of peace, calm and serenity. It contrasts with the ornate and showy style of many western cathedrals and seems so far away from the violence and aggression of the fundamentalist Islamists. The story of religious fanaticism has episodes down the ages.

The Christian crusaders who ransacked Constantinople in 1204, en route for Jerusalem on the Fourth Crusade, caused more havoc and destruction than the Islamists under Sultan Mehmet II who captured the city in 1453. In a peaceful gesture, the conqueror welcomed back Christians and Jews who had fled the city, and he began a huge restoration programme of the run-down capital of the Byzantine world, which became Istanbul.

There is much to admire in the true soul of Islam, which is belied by its warmongering modern 'Crusaders'. This is what I've learnt to respect through frequent recent visits to Istanbul.

Micro adventures

Finally, if all this adventuring is beyond your budget or not to your taste, you can always follow the advice of Alistair Humphreys, who has founded the micro-adventure movement. This Yorkshireman is a man for big adventures, having cycled 46,000 miles around the world from 2001 to 2005.

Then he got married to Sarah, who had waited patiently for him while he was globetrotting, or rather pedalling. Partly to accommodate family life with two small children, he decided some years later to go on a micro adventure in the UK, cycling around the outside of the M25 in one snowy January week.

"It felt like a big adventure," he told BBC Radio 4's *You and Yours* in January 2018, "using fields, lanes, footpaths, villages and small towns. I found wilderness places and met kind people.

"One of the joys of a micro adventure is the planning. The benefit is that it's local and simple. You have to choose your own adventure."

You don't have to follow his passion for camping in remote places and wild swimming in rivers, but you can plan and execute a micro adventure in your own favourite place, with your family if you like.

There are helpful hints on his website of locations close to London, favourite wild spots in the UK, a kit list, recipes, dealing with the elements, sleeping bags and mats, lighting fires, and much more.

He writes, "I believe that adventure is about stretching yourself, mentally, physically and culturally... Adventure is all around us at all times.

"Adventure is accessible to normal people, in normal places in short segments of time and without having to spend much money. Adventure is only a state of mind." **www.alastairhumphreys. com/**

In short, adventure through travelling helps us to recover our energy, enthusiasm and zest for life.

Next chapter, Next steps.

Start right now – It's never too late

"The secret of getting ahead is getting started."

MARK TWAIN

What I've Learnt

- Make plans
- Mind maps are a great help, as I have found with this book
- Talk to people who have taken your route
- Take action

Newly published novelist, aged 96

If you need one piece of inspiration, take the example of William Glen who had his debut novel published at the age of 96. Called *After The Panic*, it has been published under his pen name Glen Williams.

"It's exciting to have my own work available in a public space," he said. "I've had great feedback so far."

William, who spent his working life as a plumber, lives in a retirement home in Glasgow. He was inspired to write his novel after going to writing classes.

He was careful to spend months planning his book, about a dispute between South American drug barons which leads to a bomb being left on a cruise ship. The story follows three passengers who are accidentally left behind when the ship is evacuated.

William's novel has been a big hit at the retirement home where he lives. He has now finished a second book, a memoir of his time in the war in Normandy where he was wounded.

Note that William Glen followed the basic rules of fulfilling his dream:

- Training
- Planning
- Hard work

This year I have celebrated my 71st birthday, and I'm ready for new adventures and experiences. My next adventures are in Canada in August 2018 for my niece's wedding near Niagara Falls, and then Sri Lanka and eastern India in 2019.

Now, it's time to take heed of all the warnings and encouragement in this book and get down to what you have always wanted to do. You are worth it. Without question. And you are never too old.

In your heart, you know what it takes to have an adventure. So it's over to you.

What I've Learnt: Top 10 lessons

1. Communication skills require hard work, but they are invaluable.

2. Constant dialogue and listening carefully are the keys to good communication.

3. Human relationships are vital, but they remain a work in progress.

4. Emotional intelligence enhances awareness of and access to feelings.

5. Vulnerability provides the key to wholeheartedness and emotional clarity.

6. Identify one single event to understand what has controlled your emotional world. Mine was being sent to boarding school.

7. Intimacy involves good relationships – and means far more than just sex.

8. Seek and find your special niche in life. I'm keeping an open mind about what I want to do 'when I grow up'.

9. Travel and adventure are liberating. Micro adventures can be just as stimulating as big budget expeditions.

10. Make a plan, and act on it. It's never too late to try new things.

Reasons to be cheerful

There is no substitute for good communication skills, and they can be acquired with patience and persistence – as long as they involve proper listening and dialogue. At the same time, practise emotional intelligence and Goleman's main ingredients of EQ: 1. Confidence; 2. Curiosity; 3. Self-control; 4. Capacity to Communicate ("exchanging ideas and feelings with others"); 5. Cooperativeness ("balancing one's own needs with others in the group").

Feelings are prompted by present-day experiences, which evoke memories from the past and release a flood of emotional chemicals. You could have inside you the normal average of 9 feelings, according to Dr Alan Watkins, or it is possible to have as many as 34,000 (Heaven help you!). At least you can comfort yourself in the knowledge that the flood of emotions will engulf you for a maximum of 90 seconds and then pass through you, according to Dr Joan Rosenberg.

Rest assured by Brené Brown that staying open and vulnerable will bring wholeheartedness and the key to feelings. Identify that one crucial moment which upset the emotional applecart (like being sent away to boarding school), and this knowledge will provide a springboard for future fulfilment and happiness. Alternatively, seek help from a happiness coach. So, with the foundation of good relationships and courage, intimacy – or close familiarity – is only a heartbeat away.

Solitude

Remember Dr Anthony Storr and *Solitude*, and being alone. He maintains that the capacity to be alone is important for everyone, not only creative geniuses such as artists, composers and writers.

So individual passions for gardening, reading, playing the piano or watching sport are just as valuable as having satisfying relationships. People who are largely at one with themselves, with other people and with their environment, have a real chance of finding fulfilment and happiness, according to Dr Storr. In search of solitude and respite from our busy world, he advocates individual interests and meditation or prayer.

Achieving a special niche and finding new adventures are the last two pieces left to complete the personality puzzle, and then, my friends, get ready to go forth and Feel it as a Man.

BIBLIOGRAPHY

Brown, Brené: *Daring Greatly*

Goleman, Daniel: *Emotional Intelligence: Why It Can Matter More Than IQ*

Haig, Matt: *Reasons To Stay Alive*

Halford, Simon: *Intelligent Sex: Transform Your Sex Life and Relationship*

Karter, John: *Psychology of Relationships, A Practical Guide*

Harari, Yuval Noah: *Sapiens*

Mitchell, Wendy, And Wharton, Anna: *Somebody I Used to Know*

Renton, Alex: *Stiff Upper Lip*

Robinson, Ken: The Element: *How Finding Your Passion Changes Everything*

Storr, Anthony: *Solitude*

Tremain, Rose: Rosie: *Scenes From a Vanished Life*

Williamson, Marianne: *A Return to Love*

Photo: Michel Focard

ABOUT THE AUTHOR

Nick Keith is a writer and editor. Having graduated from Oxford University with a degree in Modern History, he worked for *The Times* for ten years, three as Sports Editor. Since then he has run companies producing contract books for top publishers and corporate magazines for major companies such as Eastern Electricity, Rolls-Royce Motor Cars and Sky Sports TV. As director of a marketing company, he launched three community magazines.

He lives in Winchester and has three sons, a daughter, and three granddaughters.